I finished your book in  could not put it down. It was riveting, heartbreaking, sad, disturbing, shocking, compassionate, hopeful, loving, and I could go on. I have so many emotions reeling through my head. What a life, and what a story. I didn't even know that magnitude of trauma could be experienced by one person (let alone four) over and over again.

—**Leslie Leath**

Mark has a talent that enables him to pour life into people who are dealing with the most devastating of circumstances. Whether it's debilitating physical, mental, or emotional trauma, he is always available for intentional servitude. He is able to provide a recovery filled with clarity and confidence that will allow you to prosper!

—**Steve Parker, executive director of A Happy House**

I have had the privilege of being a pastor in three different churches over the last forty-five years. I have seen and heard about every story of loss, hurt, pain, abuse, resentment, and suffering. There are very few people I have met who have experienced what Mark Goodman has experienced in life. And yet, he rose to love and grace and freedom through forgiveness. This man has been there and suffered with the greatest. Read this book carefully and prayerfully. You, too, can be free as you take good notes and do as Mark has done.

—**John Woodall, retired pastor from North Point Community Church**

I just finished Mark's book about his tragically beautiful story he was sharing with hurting people. How could I have known that his advice on guilt, blame, and shame would serve me in such a timely manner? His words acknowledge those three emotions while discouraging readers from languishing in or being defined by them. This book spurred me on to do the work required to address my responsibilities in order to move forward. Many are sure to come to know the freedom found in granting forgiveness from this former dumpster-diving beach bum.

—Ed Hardin

After hearing Mark Goodman's story and learning more about the power of forgiveness, I realized that I had much to learn. My understanding of forgiveness was transactional; something occurs. But thanks to Mark and the resources he has created about the path to forgiveness, I moved past the superficial and was able to deal with the relational issues that linger in the form of resentment, anger, shame, and a lack of trust.

—Tom Martin, board member of One Thing Ministries

Mark is a true inspiration to me and countless others with his unwavering kindness, compassion, and generosity toward others. Mark's life story is nothing short of incredible. He has overcome so many obstacles and challenges and emerged stronger and more resilient than ever before. His story shows that with hard work, determination, and a positive attitude, anything is possible. It is truly inspiring to see how Mark has turned his struggles into opportunities for growth and change, and his story serves as a reminder that no matter what life throws our way, we have the power to overcome it and come out even stronger on the other side. Mark Goodman has been and will forever be my inspiration in this thing we call life.

—Araina H.

Having shared in some of Mark Goodman's family experience, as a relative who spent time growing up with his older brother Bobby, I can say that Mark is uniquely qualified to counsel people on forgiveness based on his own ability, with God's help, to completely forgive his family. He has kindly helped me to forgive in my own family life.

—**Bud Harris**

In my lifetime, I have experienced many opportunities to forgive people for the hurtful things that occurred. I struggled with this for a year, and the most powerful moment was when Mark told his story. I was so inspired to think that God's sacrifice for our sins and our ability to love and forgive is a gift to us, not to the abuser.

—**Anonymous**

Wow, Mark! I just got a chance to listen to your talk. So inspiring, clear, and hopeful!

—**Mark Riggins, community life pastor for Encounter Life Church**

My post-divorce life was bitter and growing more resentful by the day. Anger was my friend, and a chasm of injustice separated me from happiness. I wanted positive change in my life, but the temptation of sweet revenge or numbing my pain through substance abuse was haunting and alluring. Mark's life story was the message I needed to affirm I could choose a better long-term path for my life. His life story convinced me that I, too, could become what I like to call a hero of forgiveness, free from anger. Mark taught me that the only way to bridge the injustice gap is through forgiveness. To say Mark is an inspiration is an understatement. He is one of the true heroes in my life, and because of Mark's influence, I live free and happy.

—**Dean C.**

I have thought and contemplated suicide for a long time. On the surface, it looks like I have a wonderful life, but I just have had some really bad times lately that people do not see, and I didn't want to go on. I came very close—that is, until I read your story. It said, "Suicide doesn't take away the pain; it just puts it on someone else." It really made me realize how much it would hurt my family. I'm going to work through these problems. I just thought you should know that today, you saved a life.

—Anonymous

Mark Goodman helped me with a part of forgiveness that I never knew. My daughter and I have been estranged for about twelve years. While my actions are the cause of this estrangement, I have spent most of my life trying to get forgiveness from her and restore the relationship. Because God forgave me for all of my mistakes, I had to be able to forgive her for her decision. The part that Mark helped me understand is forgiveness does not always end with reconciliation. My reward today is peace because of Mark's help.

—Doug Edwards

Forgiving a Good Man

An abuse survivor's story of freedom through forgiveness

Mark Goodman

XULON ELITE

Xulon Press Elite
555 Winderley Pl, Suite 225
Maitland, FL 32751
407.339.4217
www.xulonpress.com

© 2023 by Mark Goodman

All rights reserved solely by the author. The author guarantees all contents are original and do not infringe upon the legal rights of any other person or work. No part of this book may be reproduced in any form without the permission of the author.

Due to the changing nature of the Internet, if there are any web addresses, links, or URLs included in this manuscript, these may have been altered and may no longer be accessible. The views and opinions shared in this book belong solely to the author and do not necessarily reflect those of the publisher. The publisher therefore disclaims responsibility for the views or opinions expressed within the work.

Unless otherwise indicated, Scripture quotations taken from the King James Version (KJV)–*public domain*.

Scripture quotations taken from the Holy Bible, New International Version (NIV). Copyright © 1973, 1978, 1984, 2011 by Biblica, Inc.™. Used by permission. All rights reserved.

Paperback ISBN-13: 978-1-66288-312-5
Ebook ISBN-13: 978-1-66288-313-2
Audiobook ISBN-13: 978-1-66288-314-9

Table of Contents

1. Early Years 1
2. My Father 7
3. Key Turning Point #1—My Heavenly Father 23
4. Key Turning Point #2—Escape to Ben Lippen 33
5. Escape to California 39
6. The Painful Trip Back to Detroit 51
7. The End of Detroit; the Start of My Life 59
8. Key Turning Point #3—Unusual Path to Forgiving 67
9. Each Brother Takes a Different Path 77
10. Key Turning Point #4—Taking Off the Mask 95
11. Fork in the Road—Now What? 109

Epilogue: Freedom Found in Forgiveness 117
About the Author 127
Additional Resources 129
Notes 131

To my dad, who taught me that nothing is unforgiveable.

PROLOGUE

Why Forgiveness?

> As in a game of cards, so in the game of life, we must play what is dealt to us, and the glory consists, not so much in winning, as in playing a poor hand well.
>
> —**Josh Billings (1818–1885),**
> **American humorist and lecturer** [1]

One of the most important life lessons I learned came from my brother. We were in California, at Pirate's Cove Beach, living the life of homeless but happy young beach bums. Having no money meant we often had no food. But not to worry, my brother knew where to find all the food we might need: in local dumpsters outside of restaurants and grocery stores. His direction on how best to scavenge food from a dumpster was simple:

"Don't reach for the food on the top or the sides; the gold is in the middle, just under the surface."

Another life lesson was much more important, but that life lesson didn't come until much later in my adult life—two decades later, in fact. But just so I don't get ahead of myself, I first need to tell you my story, which is a story cloaked with pain, survival, and denial.

When my brother gave me the basic how-tos of dumpster diving, we were living as homeless young men on the streets and beaches of Southern California because we had had enough of our life back home. Ours was an all-too-common story: raised in an abusive and chaotic home, we fled to be on our own the first chance we got.

I was a typical Detroit kid just as our family was a typical Detroit family. My three older brothers—in order from oldest to youngest, Jim, Bob, and Mike—and I were raised by blue-collar parents who were veterans of the Second World War. We lived in a working-class neighborhood, my parents had working-class friends, and we attended schools filled with working-class kids. We were as Detroit as it gets: we were fans of the Red Wings, Lions, and Ford Motor Company. We dreamed of nothing but growing up and graduating with our friends and then working alongside them on one of the assembly lines, all while living in or near our familiar neighborhood. In our day, Detroit kids didn't dream of getting out.

And that's where we veered from the script.

My parents were rage-fueled alcoholics who spent their weekends getting loaded at the Moose Club, a dive bar where locals smothered their dull workweek with jokes and Jack Daniels. So regular were their drinking binges that we boys came to call them "Alcoholics Unanimous." And when they were boozed up, they went to war like only two Marine vets could. Once home, my father shouted at my mother, and my mother screamed back. Fists flew. Bruises and blood followed. In the end, the violence spread and injured everyone, especially my older brothers. I suppose Jim, my oldest brother, figured that if he was going to live in a war zone, it may as well be one of his choosing. So, he joined the Navy as soon as he could and left the house with a crew cut and a rucksack, choosing to fight battles overseas rather than fight battles at home.

Bob and Mike, too young to leave the house, each dealt with their demons in their own way. The constant chaos and the secret, incestuous sexual abuse threw both into spates of anxiety and deep depression. Bob turned to alcohol, then weed, then acid, and finally heroin. Mike did the best he could until schizophrenia took over. He left home the day after high school ended and made his way to the golden beaches of Los Angeles to escape the dullness of Detroit and the daily horrors of our home.

When my turn to graduate came, however, I made no escape. I stayed in Detroit, got a dead-end job, and found myself trudging down a long road to nowhere—that is, until my brother Mike returned from California and started telling me tales of living on the beach.

Before long, we loaded up my green 1966 Volkswagen Beetle and set off for our own adventure. But having been raised in a chaotic, violent family and not having my own coping skills meant that my little adventure would not end well. It would take many years for me to wade through the confusion, pain, and shame that stained my childhood and stole my adolescence to figure out what was missing.

That is what this book is about. It is a personal journey of freedom from pain, shame, and blame to learn about forgiving a good man. My path of freedom found in forgiveness was tough but well worth the work it required. If you are willing to follow me on this journey, your reward is a way to relate to your own pain story and to find out what is forgivable, why, and maybe even how.

As I look back now, I can see that I was doing what I could with what I had, emotionally and otherwise, and that my life's true path would not emerge until I learned the most important lesson.

But before I learned that lesson, a lot had to happen to me. And that is where I begin my story.

CHAPTER 1

Early Years

Owning our story can be hard but not nearly as difficult as spending our lives running from it.

—Brené Brown [2]

Growing up in Detroit in the seventies was an adventure all its own, with danger lurking around every corner. Every day, the streets became more dangerous. The smell of ash and smoke filled the air, a constant reminder of the automobile factories and the riots that had taken place only years before. The sounds of gunshots were familiar, ringing through the night air like a sinister chorus. The sight of abandoned and gutted buildings was also common. Every year on the night before Halloween, called Devil's Night, hundreds of homes would be set aflame for fun. Some of them would be left half-standing, the walls charred and blackened by the diabolical desire to destroy for entertainment.

In the midst of this mayhem, we lived in a 1,100-square-foot house in a blue-collar section on the outskirts of Detroit in the neighborhood of Dearborn, home of Ford Motor Company. It was a respectable place to grow up with other working-class kids. It definitely wasn't Beverly Hills, but it was still far enough from the worst of Detroit that it allowed us kids to play stickball in the street without worry. The cold reality for me was that my future held little hope of a prosperous life other than graduating from high school and doing as most responsible Detroit kids do by working thirty years on the assembly line.

I was born in Detroit in 1959, the youngest of four boys. My mom would tell me that I was the best mistake she ever made. Growing up, I was my parents' golden child, the obvious favorite as the baby of the family, which provided some shelter against the turbulent storms that continually rocked our home. Although I was granted a certain degree of respite from the worst of the damage, I was certainly not immune to it.

Dad worked at the Ford Motor Company as an office facilities manager even though he actually had a law degree from Atlanta, where he was from. Mom, on the other hand, was from Detroit. Dad was attending law school when Mom first got pregnant. He intended to pass the bar in Michigan and become a lawyer, but after the news of their first child's imminent arrival, he quit trying to become a lawyer and got a job at Ford instead. After three more children, the strain of providing for his family left him exhausted, and without the energy and resources needed to further his law aspirations, he instead remained for thirty years at Ford. No longer able to contemplate the structural complexities of plea bargaining or the finer points of contract law, his days were spent stuck in a mundane office job at the Rouge factory complex, where he spent dull days laboring under the harsh fluorescent lighting to the monotonous crunch of paperwork and reports.

We weren't poor, but we weren't children of a lawyer either. Our father was far from being kindhearted. He was often filled with a simmering rage that made the air feel heavy, and his voice could be as sharp as a blade when he spoke. His presence was so intimidating that we would often tense up and become quiet when he walked into a room, never sure what to expect from him.

The simplest way to sum up my father is to say that hurt people hurt people.

The point is my father was a troubled man.

Chaos

If there was one thing, one characteristic that defined our home life, it was chaos. Detroit was a menacing and unpredictable place, yet the chaos I encountered within our home was far more certain: an invisible tension within our home that infiltrated every corner. The outside world was a danger I could see coming, yet the danger in my home was far more insidious. Growing up with two alcoholic parents meant that chaos was everywhere. It was an abusive household, not just between my father and us kids but among us kids as well.

Both my parents had a family history of unresolved abuse, and it showed. They would get drunk at home or the bar, and then their drunkenness fueled other issues throughout our home. Eventually, we kids all dealt with this chaos in our own ways.

The moment Dad would turn the key in the door, we boys would scatter, eager to be anywhere but in the house. Desperate to avoid his presence, we would fabricate a flurry of excuses, anything to get out of the house and away from his looming figure.

Like so many alcoholics, when my dad was sober, he was a nice guy, but after that first drink, anything could happen, and most times it wasn't good. When my father got drunk, the atmosphere changed. His words became more hostile, and his demeanor more aggressive. He lashed out with his fists, leaving us in fear and trembling. His blows were so powerful that my brothers were sent sprawling, nearly knocked unconscious. In modern times, he never would have gotten away with it. It was a different time then. In today's world, when a child comes to school on multiple occasions with a black eye or bruises, the authorities are notified.

To relieve the shame that goes with abuse, we boys would have excuses for bodily damage to cover up the fatherly wounds.

At the same time, Dad never let his drinking affect his work. He never missed a day. I guess you would call him a functioning alcoholic. On Sundays, he faithfully performed his duties as an elder at the Baptist church we regularly attended despite the turmoil and chaos of the private world in the Goodman household.

The earliest memory so vividly etched in my brain is the day my second-oldest brother Bob showed me his heroin needle. His eyes were distant and deep, his hands trembling as he held it out to me. He warned me in a desperate whisper not to make the same mistakes he had. His voice, so unlike the happy Bob I knew, echoes in my head to this very day. His graphic warning etched into my mind to such a degree that it scared me from drugs the rest of my life.

When I was growing up in the late sixties and seventies, bumper stickers were beginning to be a big thing. I mention this because I had pasted bumper stickers on the outside of my bedroom door to hide the holes that my brother Mike put in the door when he came after me with a baseball bat or a knife. I can still remember the sound of the blunt thuds of his bat reverberating through my bedroom door as the hinges slowly began to give way, prompting me to consider forsaking the door and frantically devising an escape plan. I had a mere moment to react as I considered a dangerous yet desperate approach; I envisioned myself plunging through the glass and out the window, and the thought of the shards piercing my skin filled me with terror. After he finally calmed down and our argument subsided, I wanted revenge. I later exacted this revenge on him by sneaking into our shared bathroom and carrying out a vile desecration. Trembling with rage, I unzipped my fly and let out a steaming stream of vengeance right onto his toothbrush.

The next day I waited for the choice moment to tell him he had brushed his teeth with my retribution. As soon as the words left my mouth, I ran like hell as he chased me through our neighborhood. He eventually caught me and got me back good. He swung an aerosol can he was carrying, striking me in the eye hard enough to require a trip to the hospital for a half-dozen stiches. Yes, chaos and violence were common in the Goodman household.

When I was twelve, my mother was admitted to a mental hospital for what we were told was a nervous breakdown. Shortly after she returned, my father claimed that he was going to take his own life and went upstairs. I cautiously crept up to their bedroom, and there was my father, slumped over his desk with a shiny knife in his hand, trembling. His drunkenness had deafened him to my presence, so I seized the opportunity to snatch the weapon from his grasp. I raced downstairs, screaming for my mother, my heart pounding in my ears. Knowing my father's precarious emotional state, my brothers and I broke into his safe and took his handgun as a precaution. I'm not sure what Mom did or said, but by the next day, everything was back to normal—normal as defined in Goodman family terms.

Wisdom and Insight from This Chapter

Even though I don't know you, I am guessing that you have your own story of pain. Let's face it: none of us makes it through life without suffering emotional wounds and scars, some inflicted by others, some self-inflicted.

While it is impossible to know how much of my father's monstrous behavior was his own doing and how much was due to his background, we can still have empathy for an abuser like him because we choose to do so. When we hone our ability to empathize and tap into our hearts, it unleashes a tranquil cascade of understanding and warmth that lays the groundwork for our healing and forgiveness.

The journey continues . . .

CHAPTER 2

My Father

> My relationship, for example, with my father – very difficult, and very painful, and it took me 50 years to wipe the face of my father off the face of God.
> —**William P. Young, author of *The Shack*** [3]

So much of the hurt that my family and I endured over the years came from one man: my dad.

At this point, I need to warn you that this chapter describes violence, and many who read this will believe that the wrongs I recount are unforgivable. But if you are brave enough to keep reading, I hope that you will be rewarded with some lasting, positive perspectives.

My father grew up in a chaotic, abusive, and racist home environment south of Atlanta. My dad's dad was a traveling salesman. Granddad was a womanizing, heavy-drinking, smoking, tough son of a bitch. I will never know the level of abuse he heaped on my dad. I've been told that through DNA testing, it was learned that my grandfather fathered a child with his sister-in-law. I guess the apple doesn't fall far from the tree.

Dad's mother was not exactly the epitome of a southern belle. She had a chill that cut through every one of her words and gestures with a gaze like a frigid lake—emotionless and untouchable. As I remember her, she was living in Georgia in her own house with her sister. They were old-school southerners who openly spoke about having a "nigra" (as people down south often called African Americans back then) who took care of everything for the family, from cooking to cleaning. Even at a young age, whenever I heard that word and the obvious servant position she had in the home, it was like nails scratching against a chalkboard, sending a chill down my spine. But because my father was raised in that kind of environment, he never considered it derogatory.

I suspect my father's childhood was far from happy and love-filled. I have a picture of him as a young child dressed in a dress, which may have been the custom at the time when taking formal pictures of young children, or it might indicate something more sinister, but I will never know.

As soon as he could, my father left home and joined the US Marines, as World War II was then in full swing. With a chip on his shoulder, thanks to his troubled and abusive upbringing, he was soon sent off to fight in the Battle of Okinawa.

The conflict in Okinawa was the bloodiest battle in the Pacific. In the three months of the battle, more than 240,000 people lost their lives. The American loss rate was 35 percent, totaling 49,151 casualties with 12,520 killed or missing. [4] I can only imagine the sights, sounds, and smells of horror that surrounded him. He would never talk about it.

I've come to accept that my father returned from Okinawa with a spirit broken by trauma, his emotions tightly interwoven with anger and despair. The previously damaged young man had been replaced by someone hardened and consumed by a destructive reliance on alcohol to mask his inner turmoil. His capacity to cope with his emotions had been stripped away, leaving a damaged foundation for the man, father, and husband he was to become.

My Mother and Father Meet

While on leave one night in Los Angeles, my father decided to take a taxi, hoping to go have some fun and meet some girls. Right as he climbed in, another couple climbed in. Even though my father wasn't the first in the cab, he told the couple that he was on leave and didn't intend to give up the ride. They told him that they were going to the Trocadero nightclub and invited him to join them, so he did. If you haven't figured it out already, the young woman was my mother. Once at the nightclub, my mother's date, who was a Navy guy, declined to dance, so my father offered to dance with her. As the night wore on, the flirting increased. At one point, they were all sitting at a table with my mother holding the Navy guy's hand while she was playing footsie under the table with my father. I know all this because I still have the photo of the three of them taken that night. A whopping ten days later, my mom and dad were married.

What a great way to start a marriage, right? Like many wartime couples, my parents barely knew each other. When I once asked her why she married him so quickly, she said that my father was so sexy that she couldn't wait. Indeed, my father was good-looking and well-built. But marriage in ten days?

The fact is, my mother and father never should have gotten married or had kids. They were about as ill-equipped for parenthood as two people could be. But they got married and had kids, and we kids suffered the collateral damage.

Family Life and Abuse

For me, some of what I had to escape came from my brothers. The physical abuse between father and son, and even brother to brother, was out in the open.

For instance, one day, Bob and Jim got into a bow and arrow fight. Bob and Jim's bow and arrow fight was the real deal—the kind that could easily have been deadly. They stepped out to face each other, bows drawn and arrows notched. The tension between the two was evident, each determined to outwit the other as they let their arrows soar in a thrilling battle for supremacy. Amazingly, they both missed and lived to tell this story another day.

My father regularly beat my oldest brothers, Jim and Bob, often hitting them with his fists. One time my father grabbed a baseball bat from the corner of the room and violently lashed out against my brother Jim, brandishing it menacingly and striking him viciously. On another occasion, my father's rage boiled over, and he unceremoniously heaved Jim out of the living room window, sending him tumbling to the ground outside.

My cousin Bud remembers coming to a sleepover at our house and spending the night on the double bunk beds in the same room as my three older brothers. Being normal, fun-loving boys, he and my brothers were joking around and making a lot of noise. My father soon came upstairs and told them to be quiet and go to sleep. Again, being boys, they eventually got rowdy again, but this time, my father came up and beat my three brothers. As he lay on his bunk bed, my cousin could hear the thump, thump, thump of hits as my dad moved from one brother to the next, and he knew that they were much more than just slaps. After beating my brothers, my dad went over to Bud, and with a fist raised over his head, he asked him if he wanted some of the same.

He didn't lay a finger on my cousin, but the memory of that night still looms large in my cousin's memory. Despite having just been beaten, my brothers didn't cry. Instead, they whimpered quietly. My brothers had learned how to take a beating and knew that making more noise would only invite more abuse. Even after all this time, my cousin Bud, now seventy-two, can recall the terror he felt.

This same cousin fondly reminisces about the days he spent delivering newspapers alongside my brother Bob. The satisfaction of completing their route and sharing stories with each other during the ride home is a cherished memory for him to this day. One day, they were late paying for their papers, so the newspaper delivery manager called our home to talk with my father. Bob and Bud rode their bikes to our house while Bob went in to talk to my dad. Bud waited outside for what seemed like forever. Bob emerged from the house, his left eye swollen and discolored to a deep bruise, blood dripping from his split lip. He warned my cousin to leave that instant. Scared for his life, Bud took off for his home, leaving his bicycle behind. My dad took his abandoned bike and hung it up in the back of the garage, in clear sight, basically daring my cousin to come back and retrieve it. Days later, when my cousin knew my father was not home and the coast was clear, he came back and got it.

A Painful Discovery

Besides being physically abusive, my dad sexually abused all three of my older brothers.

For a little boy to be sexually violated is horrific, but to be assaulted by your own father causes unimaginable pain and lasting issues, which it did in each of my brother's cases. We Goodman boys descended into a tortured existence in which our days were filled with the oppressive weight of shame and humiliation, casting a cloak over our family no words could ever lift.

Because I was the youngest and didn't grow up with all my brothers around me all the time, I didn't discover the sexual abuse my father had inflicted on my brothers all at once. Instead, this painful knowledge came to me slowly over time. At first, I denied that it could even be true. But then I discovered what had happened to one brother, then another, and then another. I don't recall how I first heard this awful news, but I do remember that I handled it by doing what I, and my brothers, had always done with conflict: escaping both mentally and physically.

Each boy took different levels of abuse from my father—physical, sexual, emotional, and neglect. My brother Mike explained his experience of dealing with my father's sexual abuse this way:

> I *completely* relate to this subject for what Earl [our dad] did to me in my Venice Street bed from the first Monday evening of September 1966, every other night for exactly two months. I was mentally gone after Earl's first rape of me. I knew it would continue indefinitely if I did not stop him. I took a kitchen butcher knife as he sat in my bed readying to make love to me—the polite verbiage—and calmly sliced my pillow open, telling him, "If you ever touch me again, I will cut your throat open as you lay asleep in your bed, and you will bleed to death in seconds." Earl began to sob. He stated that he assumed I

was enjoying the lovemaking (his exact words) as much as he did. [5]

Living with our dad was like a black fog, oppressing us, squeezing the breath out of us, as the sickening reality of his perverse actions filled our lives, hearts, and minds.

For Jim and Bob, the sexual abuse happened almost daily for years. On multiple occasions, my father would hire prostitutes and have Jim or Bob have sex with them while he watched.

How can one forgive such a thing?

Jim talked often about his ruminating thoughts of killing our dad. Our aunt came to visit our family when Jim was young, and when she went to leave, Jim chased after her, begging her to take him with her. My brothers' nights were filled with torment, writhing, and tossing in their beds as their minds conjured the vivid and painful nightmares of our father. Not surprisingly, even after they grew up, each of them suffered variations of the same fate of nightmares, an inescapable horror that left them trembling nightly in their sheets.

The sexual abuse didn't end with my brothers. My oldest brother Jim foolishly left his daughter, my niece, at my parents' house when he and his wife left on a vacation. When alone, my father tried to remove her training bra while hugging her. Later that night, he came into her bedroom. Wreaking of alcohol, he laid on top of her and sexually assaulted her.

NEGLECT IS STILL ABUSE

As kids, we were desperate for a respite from the oppressive environment of our home. As soon as my father opened that first bottle, his demeanor would rapidly change; he transformed from Jekyll to Hyde, a figure of pure malevolence. His temper became explosive, his words acidic, and his face hardened like stone. We would escape from the home at the first sign, eagerly breathing in the fresh atmosphere to replace the vacuum my father had created.

Every Friday and Saturday night, they would come home from the Moose Club drunk from the cheap booze. If we boys were still up, we would scurry like mice when the lights came on, racing into our rooms to avoid the often brutal fights that would follow. My mother was also physically abused by my dad, but she anesthetized herself with alcohol and escaped via multiple hospitalizations for nervous breakdowns.

For our part, we Goodman boys each learned to put on our mask and pretend that all was good while inside, anger, resentment, and a need to exact some kind of payback to "make this right" chewed away at us.

Unlike many kids, I have no memories of doing stuff with my father, ever. He never came to any of my ball games, nor did he ever take me to any.

It wasn't much better with my mom. I'm sure my mother did my laundry at some point in my life, but I have no memory of that. With the pervasive neglect, I quickly learned to raise myself, and that included doing my own laundry.

My mother, father, brother Mike, and I went each summer to attend an annual Ford Motor Company outing at an amusement park called Boblo Island, which required that we ride a big boat down the Detroit River to reach our destination. Still sober, my father was the master of ceremonies. He was a consummate entertainer, a natural-born emcee with a charisma that filled the room. His jokes elicited boisterous laughs and had even the shyest in the crowd beaming from ear to ear. When the music started, he was the first one on the dance floor, spinning and twirling, getting everyone in the room up and moving. My sober father was always the life of the party with the sound of his deep, infectious laughter and the sight of him dancing. None of those laughing at his anecdotes could have envisioned the brutality he was capable of behind closed doors.

After Jim and Bob were out of the house, our family vacation consisted of summer road trips to a Holiday Inn in Toledo, Ohio. The primary source of entertainment for my brother Mike and me was the indoor-outdoor pool. Mike and I entertained ourselves while Mom and Dad drank. They were engrossed in their own world, distinctly separate from ours, and soon the glasses were drained and refilled again and again until the day's revelry had reached its end. This little excursion happened every year from the time I was nine until I was about fourteen. Obviously, we didn't do normal family-fun stuff.

A Few Bright Spots

Despite the mayhem, miraculously and thankfully, I always felt loved. As crazy and neglectful as our family was, my parents would express their love toward me. As I mentioned previously, I was always the favorite, and everybody knew it. As messed up as it may sound, my dad would also express his love to my mother too. Sometimes, my dad would come up behind Mom as she was doing the dishes, and he'd grab her butt as he mischievously smiled my way and say, "I just love this woman, and I love her butt."

My mom, Shirley Cahn Goodman, had a great, if rather dark, sense of humor that I thankfully inherited. After she married my father, she started referring to herself as an ex-Cahn. And after she had a mastectomy many years later, she joked that she now got 50 percent off the cost of her annual mammogram. At some point, she had gotten a tattoo of a rose on her butt, but she later claimed that it had originally been put on her back. Until the day she passed away, she was still able to find humor in everything. Perhaps her sharp wit and dusky comedic sensibilities were her life raft in a sea of desolation, allowing her to take solace in her jaded quips and develop a stoic resilience to the harshness of her world.

There were a few rare but funny moments, thanks in part to my dad's alcoholism. Once, while he was eating dinner while dead drunk, he fell asleep at the dinner table as he was holding a forkful of peas. He slept for what seemed like an eternity, even though it was only a minute or so, all the while keeping every pea intact on that fork. We all watched him in anticipation of what would happen next until he finally came to. And then, when he finally opened his eyes, he remembered where he was and what he was doing and continued to eat his peas as if nothing unusual had happened, never dropping a single one. If this isn't the living definition of functional alcoholism, I'm not sure what is.

FALLOUT

Sir Isaac Newton's law of motion states that for every action, there exists an equal and opposite reaction. Naturally, growing up around such violence and chaos is bound to take its toll. That was certainly true for me. My equal and opposite reaction was optimism—to dream of a better day, a better life, and hold on to that dream with everything I had.

Like many who grow up neglected in an abusive home, I desired a better day, a better place, a way out. Hope is an unstoppable force that can bring strength to the weak, courage to the fearful, and joy to the sorrowful. For me, hope was a powerful river that flowed through my darkest valleys and filled them with light. It was the constant flame in my life that never extinguished and always brought the promise of better days ahead. Give me a roomful of manure, and I'm going to look for a pony underneath—there's gotta be *something* good in there!

Even without a secure path that leads to a safer, more prosperous destination, the very notion of hope brings with it a sense of comfort, like a warm embrace from an old friend. I coped with the chaos by being overly and unrealistically optimistic. "Tomorrow will be a better day!" I would eventually grow in a more realistic hope once I found that path, but we will get to that.

One of my escapes entailed staring at the commercial airliners that would fly over our house. I would look to the sky and imagine myself being in that airplane with a sense of freedom washing over me as I drifted away from the oppressive grasp of my father and the city of Detroit.

Even though part of this optimism comes from my naturally cheery temperament, it was also a defense mechanism, a counteraction to the violence and chaos around me. Living with my father was like surfing a stormy sea of emotions. One day, we would be riding the waves of joy and harmony, and the next day, we were plunged into a dark abyss of despair and tension. My optimism calmed this unpredictable and often turbulent ride with its seemingly never-ending cycle of ups and downs.

To start with, the role I played in my family—according to the community of Adult Children of Alcoholics—was what they call the Mascot. Basically, I was the peacekeeper in our family. Besides being peacemakers, Mascots bring fun and relief to their family by being funny or cute, almost like a class clown. Mascots are also hypervigilant, and they are usually, though not always, the youngest in the family. And lastly, Mascots tend to have a short attention span.

I exhibited all the classic traits of the Mascot. As a result of being the family peacemaker, I was constantly alert for danger, both physical and emotional, and so my head was constantly on a swivel.

Growing up in survival mode; enduring violence, chaos, and neglect; and taking care of myself seemed normal to me. Thus, if I ever wanted or needed something, I got it myself. Without parental guidance, I was left to stumble blindly through life. Neglect left me with a chasm of loneliness and insecurity, forcing me to cobble together an existence that was fueled by sheer self-determination. In my mind, there's nothing that you can throw at me that I can't handle.

Another byproduct of my experience is a constant feeling of not being worthy. I've since come to know that feeling unworthy is, unfortunately, very common for those growing up in an abusive home. That feeling of being unworthy showed its ugly tentacles later in my life when I moved to an upscale, white-collar community outside of Atlanta that is basically Disney World for adults, seemingly filled with millionaires and Lamborghinis. At first, I hated it and felt like I didn't belong. I ridiculed the town and the people who lived there. Deep down, I knew that I was just a street kid from Detroit who wasn't worthy and didn't belong around all this niceness and prosperity. And someday, they would discover that I was a fraud, and I would be treated accordingly.

My Abuse Trigger — Our Fake Christmas Tree

Growing up in a home filled with fear and violence can imprint indelible memories that linger in the mind long into adulthood. The slightest reminder of those moments — the smell of a particular cologne, a certain phrase uttered in a heated moment, or the sound of a raised voice—can trigger a cascade of emotions rooted in that dark past.

It should come as no surprise to you by now that Christmas was not a happy time in the Goodman household. Any celebration meant more alcohol, and more alcohol meant more abuse. Thanks to the holiday, my folks got time off from work, and they spent that free time drinking. Even with as much healing as I've experienced and as much forgiveness as I've done, Christmas is still tough this many years later—there are still scars. And one distinct symbol of the outright neglect and abuse that I suffered (during what should have been the happiest time of the year) was the artificial tree that was erected every year in our living room. Because of his drinking, my father could never be bothered to buy a live Christmas tree. Instead, we always had to make do with the same cheap, fake tree that he had bought many years before. Every year, we assembled that same, crappy, poorly decorated, fake Christmas tree. Not surprisingly, as I aged, artificial trees were a trigger for me—a reminder of all those awful, booze-infused Christmases.

One Christmas, my wife bought an imitation Christmas tree, and it triggered me negatively at first. Buying a fake Christmas tree isn't a big deal for most people, and such a purchase wouldn't even merit so much as a Facebook post from them. In the past, an imitation Christmas tree would trigger me with the painful Christmases of my childhood, a symbol of how my family's toxicity could ruin the day that most people found joyous, Christmas.

But this time was different. I realized that I actually liked our new tree. As I did so, I came to terms with this simple but deep symbol of my abusive past; my enjoyment of our tree was tangible evidence of all the work I'd put in to be healed.

For those of us who have experienced abuse by others, the triggers that we have can seem strange to others—maybe a song, a smell, a location, or for me, a fake Christmas tree.

Mom Leaves for California

By the time I reached my teens, my brother Mike and I were pretty much the only two boys left at home. My oldest brother, Jim, had long since moved out, and my brother Bob wasn't around much, though he still lived on and off at our house.

When I was in the sixth grade, my mother up and left for California for almost two years. She needed an escape from Dad and her troubled world, so kids or no kids, she took it. I can't recall if I even saw her leave.

Back home, it was just my dad, Mike, and me. Mike was five years older and pretty much done with school, but even then, he was showing signs of schizophrenia.

By this point, I had already been mostly taking care of myself for years, but now I felt the weight of the responsibility of being the peacekeeper resting heavily on my shoulders with my mother's absence during this time. I have no recollection of her coming home, though she eventually returned.

Wisdom and Insight from This Chapter

The takeaway from this is that you must be willing to dig deep and explore the depths of your inner darkness to reach the sunny skies of liberation and absolution granted to you through the power of forgiveness.

It's been said that there are four forms of abuse: physical, emotional, sexual, and neglect. I experienced a tumultuous childhood plagued by neglect. I felt like an invisible child, my voice unheard and my presence unacknowledged.

As a child, being neglected is akin to being unceremoniously abandoned. It is a heartbreaking experience, one which leads to devastating emotional consequences. It strips away one's sense of security and belonging, continuing to haunt them well into adulthood. The psychological wounds of neglect can range from a pervasive feeling of worthlessness to a crippling fear of abandonment. It can also lead to anxiety, depression, and an inability to form healthy relationships. In some cases, it leaves scars on a person's life that last a lifetime, preventing them from finding true happiness. If you've experienced this, keep reading. This book is for you.

Often, I'll tell people I'm coaching that they will start to see signs of their healing in unusual ways. One sign might be that their relationships change and improve. Another sign might be that the very items that triggered them before now can be a sign of their level of healing. I am no different. My former trigger of a fake Christmas tree is now a symbol of progress. And now, my head isn't swiveling as much as it used to, and it feels good.

So, how can all this be forgiven? Trust me that it can. If there is one lesson I want to impart, it is this: everything and everyone is forgivable. In my case, my father needed to be forgiven not because of anything he did to make amends but *because I deserved* the resulting freedom that I gained when I forgave him. But again, before I would learn to forgive, I still had much to endure and experience.

The journey continues . . .

CHAPTER 3

Key Turning Point #1— My Heavenly Father

> Hope is a good thing, maybe the best of things, and no good thing ever dies.
> —**Andy Dufresne from *The Shawshank Redemption*** [6]

While my mom was out in California, the first key turning point in my life occurred during the summer between eighth and ninth grade. As I moved into my early teens, life was a perpetual game of hide-and-seek with my father.

When school break started in the summer of 1973 when I was fourteen years old, I went to stay with my brother Bob at an old and dilapidated farm just north of Detroit where Bob was staying with his friend Chuck Fields. I can't recall the city now, though it's probably another suburban subdivision by this point. Back then, it was just a big piece of land with a crappy house on it and some junk cars, a few of which worked. But to me, it was heavenly. The summer break provided a welcomed escape from the maelstrom of home life, delivering a tranquil refuge of reprieve and serenity. Dilapidated or not, it was a blissful oasis of peace.

Bob and I may have had a decade between us, but our similarities were striking; we shared the same sandy brown hair and easy smiles, and our personalities aligned in ways that made us feel like two pieces of the same puzzle.

Chuck and my brother taught me how to use a welding machine, which we then used to cut metal off the junk cars—remove the car body, basically—to construct a Jeep. We never did get that Jeep made, but one day as I was welding, a drop of its searing molten metal slipped off the edge and landed on the top of my foot. Even now, I can recall the sharp pain and smell of the metal that burned itself into my skin, leaving a permanent scar as a reminder.

Scar or no scar, it was cool just to hang out with my brother Bob and Chuck. It seemed to offer the promise of a new adventure, a way to leave my troubles behind and embark on a journey of discovery. It was my chance to stay up with the older boys, which was a big deal to me, and it meant escaping from our dad.

Chuck made no bones about it; he loved the Lord. Through Bob and Chuck, I met a bunch of Jesus freaks whom Chuck knew. They were Jesus-loving hippies, just hanging out. (For those of you who have seen the feature film *Jesus Revolution*, you will know what it was like.) Both *Jesus Christ Superstar* and *Godspell* had recently come out, so we all hung out and listened to those two soundtracks over and over, captivating our imagination of life with God.

Thanks to those guys, I came to know the Lord and started to form a personal relationship with Him. It wasn't about finding a religion; I was determined to establish a personal and intimate connection with the divine. I wanted to go beyond mere understanding and instead reach a level of profound connection, a spiritual bond with my heavenly Father that was tangible and indelible. I found the Father who loved and cared

KEY TURNING POINT #1—MY HEAVENLY FATHER

for me unconditionally, and when the summer was over and it was time to go back home and to school, I came home a changed person full of love, hope, and certainty that something was going to sweep me up and take me away from the hell I lived in. In a sense, I had finally found my airplane.

It seems that after all those years of looking up, the escape plane I had dreamed about had been there all along: it was God with all His love and mercy. My forgiveness from the Lord was complete and instantaneous, but it took years for me to learn how to forgive others, especially my dad.

Imagine that: how quickly I was open to receiving forgiveness from my heavenly Father but how reluctant I was to provide the same for my biological father. The irony of mercy is so unmistakable; we so desperately long to bask in the warmth of forgiveness when we are the ones in the wrong yet find ourselves reluctant to grant forgiveness to others who have wronged us. We are like a miser, guarding our mercy as if it were a hoard of gold, yet when it comes to granting it to those who have hurt us, we linger in hesitation and reluctance. Have you ever said the Lord's Prayer and spoke loudly during the part, "Forgive our transgressions," only to mumble through the part, "Forgive those who transgress against us"? Yep, all of this was me.

My acceptance of the Lord surged through me like a current of electricity, charging me with hope; I had been gifted a course to guide me, to take me somewhere I wouldn't have been able to reach on my own. My hope shone brighter than the sun, its rays of possibility lighting the way to a more promising life with my heavenly Father.

This was the first of four pivotal events of my life.

My Relationship with Jesus

I am eternally grateful not only for finding the Lord but for how and when I found Him. So many have been raised from an early age in strict or abusive religious families. For so many people raised by toxic fathers, the idea of God or Jesus conjures up a vision of oppressive control, a ghostly manifestation of their own oppressive father. They can feel the familiar tightness in their chest, the bitter taste of fear on their tongue, and the cold, pressing weight on their shoulders, all reminiscent of their struggles to survive the tyranny of their own father's reign.

Yes, I had a terrible relationship with my earthly father, but Jesus and God were never a part of that relationship. When I found the Lord, I was finally presented with a relationship with my heavenly Father, who was awesome and loved me unconditionally. He was full of grace and mercy and loved me just the way I am, with no need for me to change to have a relationship with him. New concept. Awesome.

The way I experienced it, finding the Lord was a process and not a discrete event, and for me, that process started early that pivotal summer, and it felt great. So, if you've had a bad dad, and many have, that connection to God can be tough. However, as I opened my heart to the Lord, I felt a wave of warmth wash over me. His presence was evident and tangible, like an embrace from a loving father. His love was powerful, unconditional, and completely encompassing, like a rolling thunder that reverberated through my soul. When I accepted Him as my heavenly Father, I felt a sense of awe, knowing that He was not just a distant being in the heavens but a source of constant, ceaseless love.

The Jesus freaks I met along with my brother and his friend taught me that Jesus was loving, grace-filled, and full of unconditional love. To receive His love, I didn't have to dress a certain way, be some particular person, or be perfect. I could just be me.

I am eternally grateful for this singular course correction that changed my life. From that moment onward, my life journey veered in a dramatically different direction from my brothers.

Regretfully, Bob and I were both endowed with a trait that was a discernable reminder of our upbringing, an attribute we both had become intimately familiar with. Bob and I both wore masks that covered what was going on inside. We projected an image that everything was great and we were both fine. Later in life, I was eventually able to take my mask off, but my brother was never able to do that. Bob had a larger-than-life personality; everywhere he went, people were drawn to him like moths to a flame. But below his radiant persona, he was a storm-tossed sea, a roiling cauldron of inner turmoil that nobody ever saw. That hidden tempest eventually consumed him, dragging him down to a place even he couldn't escape.

Bob was able to find Jesus and know who he was, but that was it—he never went any further. Bob never got to the point where he could forgive our father or complete the next steps. And after a year on the right path, he returned to his old ways and went back to using drugs.

Bob and Me

During that summer, Bob and I cooked up a leather business, and we would drive around Michigan and down to Ohio to go to events where we would sell our handmade leather goods. At the fairs Bob and I attended, we'd produce the leather products—belts, purses, and such—and we had a little schtick we used to draw a crowd. I'd expertly assemble the belts in a mesmerizing show for our customers. With mallet in hand, I'd juggle it between hits on the soft leather while my brother provided the sales patter, captivating our customers with the whirling display of my handiwork. In a flurry of quick and precise movements, I'd slap the belts together in record time, and then Bob offered them up for sale. Our business venture lasted well into that spring of my ninth-grade year.

Bob was the greatest salesman I've ever met. He taught me everything he knew about sales, some of which he picked up and some of which he had read in the many sales books he'd devoured.

Whenever a prospect asked Bob a question, he would always answer that question with a question to maintain control of the conversation. Sometimes, he and I would play a sales game with three stickers on each of our chests. The goal was to always keep asking the other person a question while maintaining the essence of the conversation, and if you couldn't think of a question to ask back, you lost a sticker.

According to Bob, in order to sell, I had to find my prospect's point A and point B, with point A being where they are now, and point B being where they wanted to go—or who they wanted to be. My next task was to lead them from point A to point B by showing them that what I was selling could help them do just that. I was merely providing a helping hand to aid them in their journey to a destination they already had in their sights. It was more of a service than a sale, and it was as if I were standing on the opposite side of the bridge, beckoning them to cross over and find their way.

Bob was a great listener with an ability to pick up on subtle cues. He would catch what the prospect felt and what was really motivating them, not just what they said.

Once, when I worked with him in a transmission shop, he was trying to sell this customer on replacing his car's transmission. At every step of the way, the prospect had an answer of no. The customer used every opportunity to demean his car, listing its every flaw and destroying its dignity. He told my brother he was fine just selling the car rather than getting the transmission fixed. Once Bob heard that, he went for broke and offered to buy the guy's car rather than fix his transmission. When I heard Bob do that, I thought he was crazy and almost interrupted him to remind him that he already owned too many junker cars. But Bob wasn't trying to buy another car. Once Bob started pushing to buy the man's car, the man started defending his car and arguing that it would make more sense to fix it up than sell it. Genius. Pure genius.

You can guess what happened next, of course. Once Bob got the man to start defending his own car, the sale was as good as closed. It wasn't long before the man decided to hire us to fix it. Such was the power of Bob and his ironclad sales process. Bob never played all his cards first. Instead, he always got his prospects to show their hand first, and Bob would then only play the cards he needed to win. Bob pounded all of this into my head, and thankfully it stuck.

I didn't recognize it back then, but Bob's lessons on being a good listener for sales also taught me how to be a better listener in all my relationships. Bob was always reminding me, "Listen well enough, and they will give you the keys to the kingdom. A great salesperson isn't a great talker; they're a great listener." And that notion applies to all my connections, not just sales. Thank you, Bob!

Mike Escapes with Schizophrenia

Around the time that he was finishing high school, my brother Mike started showing signs of schizophrenia, almost overnight it seemed, and his symptoms progressed over time. At first, his schizophrenia manifested itself in small, odd behaviors. For instance, if Mike went outside to the garage, he'd first put a ski mask on because he was sure the FBI was after him. Even today, he thinks he's in witness protection because he mistakenly thinks that he has witnessed a mob hit. While Mike still suffers from the condition, he has far less paranoia. Like most schizophrenics, he refuses to take medication, so he's not getting the much-needed chemical help that might otherwise bring him closer to normal reality.

Think about it. With all the abuse he went through, it's safer for him to live in an imaginary world than take the meds and live in this one. He's had nightmares about what our father did to him when Mike was twelve, which was his worst year, though, as I've indicated before, that was when he finally threatened my dad and put a stop to the abuse.

In a blind rage, Mike marched to our local high school with a gun clutched tightly in his hand, his heart pounding as he contemplated the carnage he was about to unleash. He was determined to teach the school a lesson they would never forget. Even now, Mike vividly remembers the fire that raced through his veins that fateful day, the intensity of his anger directed not toward the school but toward our father. He knows now that his fury was an expression of something else, something deeper, and that it had nothing to do with the school. Luckily, a policeman noticed him and stopped Mike before he got to the school. The officer didn't arrest Mike; he just calmed him down, took the gun, and sent him home. We obviously knew he was a troubled young man but never thought he could do such harm. To this day, whenever I hear of a school shooting, I find myself having empathy for both the victims and the shooter's family because of this experience.

Mike has a great memory to the point of almost being a savant. It is his blessing and his curse. It is a cruel irony that although his life has been a journey of more hardships than many, his mind retains it all in vivid, painful detail—a burden he cannot escape. If only fate had been kind enough to grant him a reprieve, to allow him a blessed forgetfulness of the past; instead, his sharp recall is a relentless tormenter. I can empathize with why he prefers to remain in a realm of his own creation; the solace and comfort of his own imaginings is unmistakable. I can feel the intangible sense of safety and security he finds in his escape from reality, and it is in this understanding that I know why he prefers the world in his mind.

For me, my escape was hope. For Mike, it was an imaginary world with emotional walls to protect him from the memories of the past. His emotional walls feel safe, secure, and free from the outside world's cruelty.

Wisdom and Insight from This Chapter

Not surprisingly, many of those people with childhood abuse from their father find it difficult to have anything resembling a personal relationship with God or Jesus. Just like William P. Young, they may need fifty years to get the face of their father wiped off the face of God. People who have been abused by their earthly father, whatever kind of abuse that was, feel pain even if they merely hear the words *heavenly Father*.

One way to look at this experience is that my bad father helped me find Jesus. This he did by creating such a hole in me that I needed desperately to fill it, and when I was introduced to Jesus, the void was filled.

The journey continues . . .

CHAPTER 4

Key Turning Point #2— Escape to Ben Lippen

What makes you magnificent is everything you've previously believed is wrong with you.

—**Cheryl Hunter** [7]

My spiritual awakening and the warm, comforting embrace of emotions I experienced over the summer at the farm with my brother Bob were awe-inspiring, but it inevitably had to come to an end. There was a pang of sadness in my heart since I wished I could stay longer and bask in the serenity of that safe and loving environment. As the sun set on this summer oasis, it was time to bid farewell to the dilapidated farm and travel back home to set my sights on the upcoming school year. However, I left gifted with the golden warmth of understanding, strength, and hope that forever resonated within me.

Now being in the ninth grade, I would leave gospel tracts about Jesus around in classes as I tried to influence my schoolmates. My mother, who was back home from her temporary exodus to California, intently observed the transformation that had taken place within me and was filled with a newfound optimism for my future.

I heard about a cousin who was enrolled in a Christian boarding school by the name of Ben Lippen located in Asheville, North Carolina. Everything about the school and its location sounded awesome to me. I thought it might be an opportunity to escape both Detroit and my family, and it would also give me a chance to hang out with other like-minded kids who believed in Jesus and wanted to talk about Him. Most of all, it would be my shot at having a great life.

The tuition was $2,000 per year, which might as well have been $200,000. My mom was working at a Fotomat store to bring in some extra cash, but her income wouldn't be enough to cover the tuition. So, she applied for a grant to help defray some of the costs, and I was accepted. Thus, in the tenth grade, I was off to a boarding school in North Carolina.

At last, I was actually inside the airplane that had been the symbol of my hope-filled dreams for so many years, the lofty metal bird that promised liberation from the Goodman home and a gateway to boundless opportunities. It was my first time ever flying, and I finally would get to explore a world of fresh possibilities.

Like the school's mission, I was full of hope and wanted to save the world. Thankfully, my mom bought into all of it to help me escape—for a time.

Asheville was—and is—a beautiful town, famous for housing the US's largest private residence, the Vanderbilt mansion known as Biltmore, which sits atop a mountain overlooking the city. The contrast between the harshness of Detroit and Asheville with its exquisite mountains and southern hospitality was almost too good to be true. This new environment enveloped me with serenity, structure, and tranquility. The experience was exhilarating!

KEY TURNING POINT #2—ESCAPE TO BEN LIPPEN

Going to a private boarding school provided me with a chance to reinvent myself. There, no one knew about my awful family or my own issues. All day long, I could play the part of a normal, happy person while keeping my family demons locked deep inside. While I did feel guilt that I was leaving Mike behind to deal with our family by himself, life at Ben Lippen was great, and I ate it up.

School was full of rules and discipline, and I loved every minute of it. The school had many traditions and strict rules that prohibited dating, touching the opposite sex, and listening to rock and roll, among other things. Basically, it was an extremely conservative institution.

The atmosphere was one of strict order and propriety. During dinner time, all the boys were required to be adorned in coats and ties, a symbol of respect and order. I suddenly had to contend with two forks, one long and one short. I was fifteen years old, but because of my dysfunctional upbringing, I had never seen both a salad and entrée fork together before. There was a complete rule book that covered everything, including how to butter and eat your bread ("Break the bread in half and butter it and eat it before you butter the second half, eating that half in no less than three bites.")

The teachers were strict too. I remember my English teacher told us that if we allowed a comma splice (two complete sentences joined by nothing more than a comma), she would stop reading our paper at that point, give it an "F" grade, and send it back.

Every day we had Bible study, followed by dinner, where they taught us to seat the young women to our right—by pulling out their chairs for them—before seating ourselves.

Ben Lippen was a high school only, educating grades nine through twelve. Its student body was evenly divided between missionary kids

(MKs), preacher kids (PKs), and ordinary kids (OKs) like me. Yes, I was finally OK in more ways than I hoped for.

Coming as I had from a totally formless and chaotic environment, the discipline was calming, reassuring, and gave me direction. Attending the school taught me that there was more than one way to do things in the world and that my crazy family and Detroit were not how life or the world functioned.

My glorious time at Ben Lippen was a lot of firsts for me. It was my first time living away from home, my first time living in a disciplined environment, and my first airplane ride. I got a chance to escape and be a new person, coupled with a fortified sense of hope that there was a better world out there. And once I tasted that, I was hungry for more.

Leaving That Christian Boarding School

I spent my entire tenth and eleventh grades there, but that's where the dream ended. In the eleventh grade, I got myself a girlfriend, and near the end of that school year, we were caught kissing. It was almost unfathomable to me that something as innocent and sweet as a peck on the lips could cause such a turbulent stir. It was as if the school faculty had just witnessed a heinous crime.

I wasn't kicked out, but they told me I wouldn't be coming back for my senior year. My girlfriend received similar immediate restrictions, but since she was a senior, she was able to graduate at the end of that school year.

Back to Detroit and Chaos

After I was told not to come back to Ben Lippen, I returned to Detroit and family chaos for my senior year of school. When I got back, Mike was no longer around because he was living as a homeless beach bum on the golden beaches of Los Angeles, the only place he knew (from television and movies) that promised a respite.

On my eighteenth birthday, in February of my final year in high school, I eagerly attended a party to celebrate my adulthood. It was the first time I ever drank alcohol, and I did so to the point of getting plastered. And of all things to choose, I drank sloe gin fizzes. The sensation of being drunk was disorienting; my vision blurry, I felt like I was in an altered reality, one in which I was adrift from the life I had been living prior. That night, I jettisoned my direction in life and Christian beliefs to embrace all the world had to offer.

Graduation was anticlimactic for a Detroit kid whose only expectation was to work on the manufacturing line. The hope for a future that once kept me going was gone. I was lost and would be for a while, which explains what happened next.

Wisdom and Insight from This Chapter

In most cases, running away from your difficulties never solves anything except a new view out the front door with the same issues you left with. It's often better to confront them head-on. However, if you are in an abusive situation, it is essential to take steps to protect yourself, which may include leaving your environment or the relationship to ensure your safety and well-being. Spending time with those who are filled with positivity and unconditional support is often what is needed to ignite the fires of forgiveness. Surround yourself with those who offer hope and love, and it can be just the spark you need.

The journey continues . . .

CHAPTER 5

Escape to California

People don't fake depression. They fake being OK.
—**Abhysheq Shukla** [8]

I don't know for certain when or how, but I knew from a very early age that I, too, would leave Detroit as soon as I could.

Like almost all my peers, I had no college or career plans. Instead of leaving right after I graduated high school, I followed most of my buddies into their rut when I took a job on the line at the Ford Motor glass plant. In no time, I had settled into the working-class rhythm, spending my weekdays working at a glass factory job that I hated and partying on the weekends, basically rolling along a conveyor belt to nowhere.

For nine months, I clocked in and out of that glass plant, watching sheets of glass flow then solidify before being cut by automated machinery. For nine months, I moved those cut sheets of glass into crate after crate. It was monotonous, dangerous work. And for nine months, glass snapped, shattered, and scattered down the line every day. They cut my shirt and jeans to ribbons. Sometimes, they sliced my hands down past the muscle. During my short time there, I watched worker after worker lose skin, digits, and self-respect. It was the seventies, and it felt like management cared more about efficiency than they did about worker safety. As the months passed, my nine-to-five life came into full focus: a hazardous, ungratifying grind, the sort of pain-filled existence endured by people who didn't have the gumption to get out.

Mike, now suffering from schizophrenic delusions, eventually returned from California. We commiserated regularly, but mixed in with our tales of daily woe, he shared stories of his time bumming on the beaches of California. He'd met good friends out there, including "a couple Jesus freaks," he said. In California, he came and went as he pleased, slept where he wanted, ate when he wanted, and worked when he wanted. In his version of California, there were no dead-end jobs, no occupational hazards, and no shards of glass. Best of all, his California held no reminders of the abuse we suffered growing up. "It was freedom," he said. The more stories I heard, the more I dreamed of getting out.

Finally, one afternoon, I had had enough. "All of this," I said as I waved my hands in the air, "means nothing. We're going nowhere. Let's get out of here!" He agreed but said he'd always wanted to see New York City, and if we were leaving Detroit, we might as well take the long way and visit the Big Apple along the way. I had been taking the long way just about as long as I could remember, so his plan made sense to me.

Three weeks later, we loaded my green 1966 Volkswagen Beetle with all our worldly possessions and brought along a combined bankroll of $330. Once in New York City, we made our way first to the World Trade Center and took the elevator to the top floor. We budgeted one dollar a day for food and nothing for lodging, so after our viewing tour, we pitched our pop-up tent wherever we had the best chance of not getting arrested. Our camping gear consisted of our tent, two sleeping bags, a couple of water bottles, and a portable gas stove. We didn't pitch on the Plaza, but we got close. Our food—mac and cheese, peanut butter sandwiches, and ramen cooked over a portable stove—was no Tavern on the Green, but it tasted just as divine to us.

From New York, we drove to Florida, where my trusty Beetle started dropping fourth gear. We rigged it with a cheap but heavy-duty rubber strap and some duct tape and then headed west. As we drove through Texas, it seemed as if the state would never end. The eternal drive made me dead bored. Finally, I took action to break the monotony. As I drove down a long stretch of interstate highway, I said to Mike. "Put your foot on the gas pedal." He did. "Now, hold the steering wheel," I added. And with those two moves, my brother, who was seated in the passenger seat, was now driving our VW bug.

The car hummed down the highway as Mike took the control of the car, and I knew I had to act fast. I slung my body out the window and wriggled onto the top of the car, feeling the gusts of wind whipping around me. We were barreling down the interstate at 55 mph, waving at the bemused people driving near us, our reckless adventure unfolding before us. Looking back, I know it was stupid, but in the moment, I felt nothing but exhilaration. The sensation of the wind whipping through my hair and the view of the world zipping by beneath me—it was like I was flying! Getting back down and into the driver's door window in a little VW bug was a different story, but eventually, I managed to land back in the seat, alive and safe with stories to tell. As you may have guessed, my crazy stunt didn't faze my brother one bit because he, too, had grown up surrounded by chaos.

Doing stupid stuff like that was partly a byproduct of my age and definitely a sign of where my head was at—and for a good part of my life thereafter. I was clearly quite comfortable with risky behavior, and it showed. I was more comfortable being on the edge of a cliff than dwelling safely on solid ground. I guess that's all I knew.

In Arizona, we took an exit for the Grand Canyon, where we pulled off and walked to the railing on the canyon's edge. While I was looking down at the Colorado River so far below, Mike hopped the rail, jumped, grabbed a tree branch that hung over the Canyon, and turned to me to yell, "Mark, throw me the camera!" The normal, non-chaos-addicted folks around us screamed, convinced my brother was trying to commit suicide. For a moment, I just stared at him. Then I shouted back at him, "You can die if you want, but you're not taking my camera with you!"

I walked back to the car and calmly waited for Mike to climb into the passenger seat. Mike's antics hadn't fazed me in the least either—I just didn't want him to include my camera in his nonsense. In silence, we continued west.

As we crossed into California, we lost fourth gear completely. We chugged our way in third gear across the desert and into Los Angeles, nearly running out of gas just as we reached Malibu Beach. We unpacked the car as the sun went down and set up camp. We had run out of money the day before and now only had a ten-cent, no-name box of macaroni and cheese to split between us. Mike lit our cheap gas stove as a chilly Pacific wind blew in. He filled a pot with cold water and macaroni, but before the water could even reach room temperature, the stove's fuel ran out. Lacking any extra gas or money to buy more, we sat and waited, hoping our macaroni would somehow soften to the point of becoming edible. It didn't.

Two hours later, we drained the water and mixed in the processed cheese powder. I crunched through my portion of dehydrated, cheese-powdered noodles as best as I could. While Mike finished his macaroni, I crawled in my sleeping bag on the beautiful Malibu beach. Wide awake and hungry, I wondered if I had made a mistake. I knew better, though. After all, I was with older brother Mike, the most resourceful human I'd ever met. Heck, the guy had turned beach bumming into an art form.

Early the next morning, Mike began showing me the ropes, including how to make a few bucks doing day labor or giving plasma. That first morning, we joined a landscaping crew for a day's wage and worked till the sun went down. At the end of the day, the foreman handed each of us a twenty, and we took our cash to a local diner. After enduring forty-eight hours with nothing to eat other than those crunchy cheap noodles, we indulged in the daily special, savoring every flavor and texture as we ravenously devoured every last bite. It was heavenly. We then took the little bit of leftover cash and invested it in staples—more mac and cheese, fuel for the stove, and gas for the Beetle.

On the days we couldn't find work, Mike taught me how to turn a casual beach friendship into a shared meal. He taught me the lucrative opportunity to donate plasma twice a week, providing quick and easy cash. He showed me the way to all the open soup kitchens and food pantries too, as well as their hours of operation. He also trained me how to find odd jobs and survive on less than a dollar a day.

Although we went on multiple occasions, I recall one particular trip to the soup kitchen in downtown LA. Here I was, this naïve midwestern kid, learning the art of living homeless, standing in line with about fifty other people. Suddenly, about fifteen people in front of us, a guy turned around and shouted, "Mike!" Here we were, standing in a random soup kitchen line in downtown LA, and some guy knew my brother! Crazy.

Now when I volunteer to serve at a soup kitchen, it takes me right back to being that lost teenager standing in line with my tray getting a meal at that downtown LA soup kitchen.

But it wasn't all hustle and survival.

Mike also taught me how to blow off steam by bumming beer from folks around campfires. It was common for beachgoers burning logs on Malibu Beach to share a joint, and I happily engaged in their generosity. Shortly thereafter, I smoked some weed that I didn't know was laced with something that almost did me in. Mike knew the cure for that too. Turns out coffee and sleep can work wonders for a bad trip.

Mike taught me how to bum SoCal beaches in style, but as valuable as these lessons were, perhaps the most important lesson, which I've already hinted at, was one that he taught me inland: proper dumpster diving etiquette. A week into our adventure, we drove around the backside of a supermarket in the town of Malibu. There, in the shadow of the large square building, Mike approached a dumpster and threw the lid back. "There's an art to this," he said as he pointed to the dumpster. "You never want to go for the easy stuff, like the stuff on the top or the sides. That's the food exposed to the air, and it rots the quickest."

He pulled a wilted and slimy leaf of rotting lettuce off the top and waved it in the air.

"See," he said before tossing it to the asphalt. He dug down farther, maybe another foot.

"If you dig down past the top, there are rows and rows of good stuff in the middle. It's the sweet spot—protected. The food on the top and sides surround it, forming a sort of dumpster cooler. It keeps the food fresher. That stuff's dumpster gold."

He reached in, pulled out an unopened package of bologna, and tossed it to me.

"Try it," he said.

He was right. It was delicious. Though maybe too old to sell in a grocery store, it was still plenty edible. As hungry as I was, it tasted delightful.

As the days passed, these grocery store dumpsters became our go-to source for meals. Sure, the food was cast off and pungent at times, but did it matter? Most of it was fit for a king as far as I was concerned. Don't feel sorry for me. I actually *gained weight* eating those Malibu food cast-offs! Even now, years removed from dumpster diving, I still remember that trash bin grub fondly because it had kept me, and hope, alive.

Another food-gathering tactic I learned involved stealing food from a grocery store while shopping. In this case, I would walk around the grocery store, pushing a shopping cart while gathering the ingredients I needed for my meal, most often a sandwich. I would open the mayonnaise jar, spread some on the bread from a loaf I had picked up, add my meat and whatever else, and then eat my sandwich as I walked around the store, still pushing my cart. Once I was done eating, I would quietly and carefully return the items—the opened mayo jar, the rest of the loaf of bread, and so on—to their places on the shelf. All finished eating, I'd walk out of the store with a full stomach and not having spent a penny. It was survival of the cleverest.

When you are hungry, it is amazing what you will do. To this day, when I see a homeless person, I wonder, *Is that me?*

The days in Southern California turned into months, and those months began to add up. We moved from beach to beach, location to location, sometimes sleeping in parks or hidden public courtyards. We kept working the campfires and bumming beer, weed, and food from anyone willing to share. We picked up day labor when we could and often ate in soup kitchens around LA.

After many months of day labor jobs here and there, just enough to keep us fed, Mike and I found regular work at the Van Nuys airport. We slept in a park in Encino and joined up with the labor crew in the mornings. In those days, we spent our cash wages well, eating whatever we wanted—burgers, deli sandwiches, and blue-plate specials. The day labor also kept gas in our car and paid for the various sundries we needed. Alas, our "season of plenty" eventually came to an end when the day labor dried up.

After a time, Mike and I decided to part ways. We hadn't argued or fallen out or anything like that. Mostly, we wanted to go to different places and wanted different things, both geographically and in life. Plus, I had grown a little tired of hanging with Mike and just needed a break.

For instance, one day we went to an ice cream shop. While there, I had befriended a nice young lady. She was too young to date but provided some greatly needed conversation. As we were chatting, Richard Mulligan, one of the stars of the TV sitcom *SOAP* (Mulligan played the deep-voiced and continually perplexed husband), came in to get some ice cream. Mike had been sitting out in the VW, eating some cottage cheese and drinking a quart of milk. Mike spotted Mulligan walking in and came barreling into the store, still carrying his cottage cheese and milk, fawning over him and peppering him with questions mixed with, "Oh my God! Oh my God!" All I could think was *No, Mike, don't*. Eventually, Mike shoved his quart of milk under his arm so he could shake the actor's hand. I was beyond embarrassed. Thankfully, Mulligan was finally able to leave in one piece.

So, we parted ways. Mike took the car and landed somewhere south of LA. I found my way to a nude beach called Pirate's Cove Beach, just outside of Malibu. Instead of confronting my issues or seeking wisdom from the Lord, I sought refuge in whatever form of escape it took.

Pirate's Cove was fun, and it yielded some interesting moments. Once, I was shopping in a store near the nude beach when I recognized the lady behind the counter, who also recognized me. I was trying to figure out where I knew her from when she started to shush me. At that moment, I realized where: I had seen her in the buff at that beach. At that point, I quipped, "I'm sorry, but I didn't recognize you with your clothes on!"

It was on Pirate's Cove beach among all those free-spirited sunbathers that the itch for home hit me hard. I can't say exactly why. Perhaps the nakedness there had exposed me as well: no home, no job, no money, and no friends. The life I was leading was unsustainable. And because Mike and I were no longer hanging with each other, I no longer had my crazy-but-resourceful older brother to guide me. I'd left my working-class monotony and the memories of my abusive upbringing for a new life in California, and it had delivered. My time homeless in the Golden State was one of relative peace and ease, especially when compared to growing up in Detroit. Maybe I had hoped California would be permanent, but I knew that I needed more than bumming the beaches for the next fifty years, if I could survive that long. Was my life plan to live on beer, buds, dumpster diving, and ten-cent mac and cheese? I had more sense than that.

I couldn't keep living on the streets and beaches of LA, even if Mike could. Maybe I wasn't delusional or carefree enough—who knows? No matter the reason, my thirst for adventure had been quenched, and perhaps I just needed to grow up. Either way, I could no longer deny the gravity that pulled me back to dead-end Detroit.

I was also nineteen years old, a baby adult. Where else was there to root down but back home?

One evening, as the sun set, I noticed a plane flying over the beach. It was a passenger plane, just like the hundreds that had flown over my childhood home, cutting clouds in half while I dreamed of riding in the cabin, escaping the violence that saturated our house. That evening, I once again found myself transported by watching that plane. Only this time, I imagined myself in the cabin heading back *home*.

Maybe it was better now. I thought of my mother, whom I'd spoken to only once since I'd left. I remembered her always trying to do right by me, even on her drunkest days. I remembered my practical and hard-working brother Bob. Last I saw him, he was doing better, and I knew he was running a transmission shop in the old neighborhood. Ah, the old neighborhood. I thought of it along with my old friends and the all-too-familiar factories. In the nostalgia of that moment, I made my decision: I would leave the beach, the day labor, and my beach friends and head back home.

Wisdom and Insight from This Chapter

With the benefit of decades of hindsight, I now realize what was happening. Raised in chaos, I'd never been comfortable with stability. I was addicted to chaos, though I didn't know it then.

It was unfathomable that the unforgiving streets and beaches of California could be a safer refuge than the home I knew in Detroit, yet inexplicably, the warmth of the sun-soaked sand and the carefree existence provided a comfort that I craved. I have good memories of my time there; however, I struggled to outrun the emotional tumult that had become entrenched in my life that seemed to follow no matter where I went. Until recently in my path to forgiveness, I would still default to chaos over equilibrium. As chaotic as being a beach bum might seem to most people, to me, it had all become too predictable, too stable, and too even keeled.

If you've been hurt, you've been running from dealing with the pain, and you are at a crossroads to forgive or not, are you ready to face and work through this issue? If so, the exploration of healing and growth awaits.

It sounds crazy, but even though I was a homeless beach bum, my life had yet to fall apart. Not even close.

The journey continues . . .

CHAPTER 6

The Painful Trip Back to Detroit

Be careful who you trust, the devil was once an angel.
—**Ziad K. Abdelnour** (9)

And so, at summer's end in 1978, I packed my bags and started to hitchhike by myself back to Detroit. Looking back, doing what I did was incredibly risky and foolish. No one other than my schizoid brother knew that I was hitchhiking alone from LA to Detroit. Given the era, I had no cell phone and no real way to contact anyone should things go south. Were I to be murdered or die accidentally, my friends and family wouldn't even know where to start looking for my body, let alone know that there was a body to find. I suppose on some level, I knew how vulnerable I was and the risk I was taking because that frame of mind influenced me when I endured the next pivotal trauma in my life. At the same time, never would I have thought that what would soon happen to me along the way would take me back to the darkest moments of my childhood.

But for the moment, I needed to get going, and sure enough, a passing car soon pulled to the shoulder, gravel crunching under its tires. I had taken the northern route across the country because I thought it would be more interesting and because it was still warm enough to do so. The driver rolled down his window to tell me he could take me as far as San Luis Obispo. I nodded, thanked him, and climbed in, taking with me a backpack carrying a total of $20 out of our precious and limited budget, a loaf of bread, a jar of peanut butter, and two cans of pork and beans.

Once in San Luis Obispo, I began hitchhiking for my next ride, heading toward San Francisco. As I started hitchhiking, I noticed that I wasn't alone in my pursuits. On almost every corner, I could see other young people hitchhiking everywhere, most going the same direction as me.

It was getting late on Saturday, so I ended my hitching and decided to camp out under the stars and sleep. The next morning, I would start back hitchhiking—there was so much competition for rides that I figured I might as well wait until then. I found a spot beneath a towering oak and tossed my sleeping bag down on a soft bed of grass, a perfect bed for the night. Walking to my mini-campsite, I happened to step in a ditch full of water. I took off my wet shoes, socks, and pants and hung them in a nearby tree to dry out. The next morning, I awoke to the sound of voices. It turned out that I had chosen to camp on the lawn of a church. Because it was Sunday morning, I was now witness to scads of people coming in for the morning service, all of whom had to walk by me as I slept on the ground—still in my underwear—next to a line of trees on the church's lot. Being without my pants, I hopped in my sleeping bag over to the tree to retrieve them now that they were hopefully dry. I dressed quickly, trying to avoid looking at the people I figured must be gawking at the half-naked young man.

After I packed up, I again headed out quickly, going back to the chaos I didn't know how to live without and into an experience that would define and shape the rest of my life.

THE PAINFUL TRIP BACK TO DETROIT

SEXUALLY ASSAULTED

I eventually made it as far as Cheyanne, Wyoming, via multiple rides along the way.

Hitchhiking was tricky. Each state was a little different regarding what they allowed you to do to snag a ride from a stranger. I learned this in Wyoming, where a highway patrolman told me, in no uncertain terms, that if he saw me put my thumb out or hold up a sign, he would take me to jail. Those activities weren't allowed in Wyoming, it seemed, and doing so meant risking arrest and imprisonment.

Not being able to hitchhike in the usual way, I got creative. In Wyoming, I tried to attract attention—and sympathy—by juggling at the side of the freeway, all done to hopefully score a ride.

My hitchhiking had taken me this far, and there I stood, by the side of the road, all day, having started early in the morning. The day passed, the sun began to set, and yet here I was still in the same spot. I recalled seeing a truck stop a mile or so back, so I turned around and walked back, hoping to hang out there. I was going to eat what little food I had left, refresh myself, and hopefully score a ride.

I had left California with my meager resources, which were now beginning to run out. There I sat in the truck stop diner, tired and hungry, asking the waitress for more hot water, hoping to squeeze all I could out of the single tea bag I had, all the while trying to figure out how I was going to find my way back to Detroit.

It had been over twenty-four hours since I last slept. (Generally, drivers don't like picking up hitchhikers at night, and when they do, you as the hitchhiker had to stay awake to make sure you weren't attacked or robbed or worse.)

While sitting alone with my backpack at that truck stop, two really nice cowboys spotted me. They chatted me up, and I soon revealed that I was headed to Detroit. I was obviously tired and looked destitute. Even if I hadn't told them, they would have easily spotted my desperate situation. They told me that they couldn't take me to Detroit, but they were happy to get me a hot meal, a shower, and a good night's sleep before I set back out on the road.

This was music to my ears, and I eagerly accepted their apparent hospitality. They soon took me back to their house, which was in a small, suburban neighborhood outside Cheyenne. It didn't strike me as strange, but soon after we arrived at their house, one of the cowboys took off, leaving the two of us behind. Looking back, I probably should have noticed that.

The cowboy who stayed fed me a wonderful meal of cooked venison. He put my clothes in the wash and let me take a hot shower. As I ate, clothed in nothing but a bathrobe, I glanced around my surroundings and noticed that one or both of them were hunters—guns and animal trophies lined the walls.

I sat there at their dining room table, half-asleep with a full stomach, when all of a sudden, the cowboy came up behind me and started rubbing my shoulders.

I woke up quickly because I now knew that I was in a deep mess.

Remember, this was back in the day when there were no cell phones and thus no easy way for me to call someone and tell them where I was and what might soon be happening to me. No one but my brother back in California knew that I was on the road, hitchhiking across the country, going from California to Detroit. There were thousands of miles and multiple routes from California and Detroit. Had anyone asked Mike where I was, he would have been able to say only that I had left within the past couple months and was somewhere between California and Detroit—he wouldn't even know which route I had taken.

Forget about even finding my body; it would be weeks or even months before anyone figured out that I was even missing.

I was in deep trouble, and I knew it.

I won't go into graphic detail of what happened next except to say that the cowboy sexually molested me.

Later that night, I was overcome with enough exhaustion that I was finally able to fall asleep on the couch in the living room. At about 4:00 a.m., I woke up and looked over only to see the same man sitting in the chair next to the couch, just sitting there watching me in the dark. I was frozen in terror and felt like I was living through the most terrifying nightmare or horror movie imaginable. For what seemed like forever, he sat there and watched me, knowing that I was awake. The silence between us hung thick in the air like a heavy fog, and I could almost feel the electricity radiating from him as he did nothing but stare at me. At that point, I started to think that I was going to be killed.

He eventually got up and left the room, but afraid for my life, I never went back to sleep and counted the minutes until the sun finally came up. In the end, though, he spared me. Early in the morning, his buddy came back, and they high-fived as he let his buddy—probably his partner—know that "all went well."

They were *nice enough* to drop me off at the Cheyenne bus station. Once there, I called my Grandpa Cahn in Detroit and pleaded for him to get me back home. "Please, don't ask me any questions," I told him, "but I'm in Cheyenne, Wyoming, and I really need you to go down to the bus station and get me a one-way bus ticket from Cheyenne to Detroit."

My grandfather soon wired me a bus ticket, and I boarded a bus back home to Detroit and my familiar chaos.

On the long bus ride home, I began to think of it as less of a sexual assault—even though it was—and more as an instance of my missing the many cues along the way. "Mark, you stupid idiot!" I said to myself many times as I recalled all the signs and warning bells that I had missed. I had been hit on and propositioned plenty of times while I had been beach bumming in California, and I had never once walked into any situations that I knew were traps. But this time . . .

That was the last time I ever hitchhiked.

Wisdom and Insight from This Chapter

People have asked me why I didn't report them, hoping to find some justice or at least prevent them from doing such a thing to another unsuspecting traveler. I might have, but for the life of me, I had no idea who they were and where that house was. Afterward, I often second-guessed myself, thinking that I could have been more forceful or could have dashed out the front door and run to a neighbor for help or something.

My reaction, to blame myself, is common in survivors of sexual assault. But the fact of the matter was that I was scared, and I did what I did to survive. I was in a vulnerable position, and I did what I had to do to make it out alive. Speak to someone who has been sexually molested, and they will tell you that they often bear partial responsibility for the abuse because of what they did or didn't do, what they were wearing or weren't wearing, or because they knowingly put themselves in the wrong place. Nonsense. When you are abused, you are not to blame. The good news is that when you forgive your abuser, you are also better able to forgive yourself for whatever you *think* you did—or didn't—do to cause the abuse.

Victims of abuse often do not report it out of fear of retaliation, disbelief, and shame. Victims may fear that they will not be believed, that they will be blamed for the abuse, or that the abuser will hurt them further if they come forward. They may also be embarrassed and ashamed of what happened to them and feel like they are to blame for the abuse. Additionally, victims may not know where to turn for help or what resources are available to them.

In a perfect world, I would love to know who those cowboys from Cheyenne are and would love to take them out for lunch—and I'm buying. I want to let them know how it hurt but also how I'm turning what they did to me into something good. I would wish them all the best. I'd be as sincere as can be. I don't harbor any ill will toward them at all.

The beauty of freedom and forgiveness is that I am a free man.

The journey continues . . .

CHAPTER 7

The End of Detroit; the Start of My Life

> Anger is an acid that can do more harm to the vessel in which it is stored than to anything on which it is poured.
> —Seneca the Younger [10]

Back in Detroit, I needed a place to stay. I didn't want to live at home, but being short on cash, I couldn't afford even a modest apartment. Luckily, a buddy loaned me enough money to buy a VW bus, which I lived in for a few months in a K-Mart parking lot until I had enough money to get a roof over my head before winter came.

With all that had happened, I couldn't see that I was a troubled young man because I thought that living in a VW bus in the K-Mart parking lot was a step up. If only I could go back and talk to that young man and get him to understand that there is freedom and a better life through forgiveness. But before that young man would figure it out, he would have to learn a few more tough lessons.

Working at Vernors

Soon after arriving back in Detroit, I got a job at the Vernors Ginger Ale bottling plant in Cass Corridor. In those days, it was one of the roughest and poorest areas of Detroit, and in the seventies, it was known for drugs and prostitution.

The work I did at Vernors was typical boring assembly line work. My job was to stand there, watching cans of ginger ale go by all day to make sure they were properly aligned before they would get flipped over to be filled. And that's what I did, hour after hour, day after day, next to the guy who palletized the cans.

To relieve the tedium, my work buddy and I would eat pot brownies and drink vodka-laced OJ throughout our shift. We would both be completely intoxicated as the brownie and OJ concoction lifted us up, higher and higher. I'd sit there as still as a statue watching the unfilled cans dance by while he operated the humming machinery with amazing precision.

One day, something went wrong with a pallet in the machine that my work buddy was operating, so he called me over to help him. While the machine was still running, I stuck both of my arms into the machinery to straighten the pallet. In an instant, my friend's finger flew to the stop button, just as two hulking metal plates were about to squeeze together and crush my arms. If he had hesitated another fraction of a second, both my arms would have been severed cleanly between my forearms and wrists. Instead of recoiling in terror, we both laughed about what had just happened. The next morning, after I sobered up, I realized how close I had come to losing both hands.

Addicted to Chaos

For most of my life, I lived on the edge of a proverbial cliff, and I preferred it that way. It's only later in life with thanks to my forgiveness journey that I've become comfortable living in peace. Prior to this change, my addiction to danger and chaos would show up repeatedly in my personal life and professional life. In my business, I would take huge risks; if I saw an opportunity, I would go all in. *To hell with living quietly and working for a pension. We're going to bet it all—now!*

I should have been content at Vernors. My bills were getting paid, and I could chill out all day at work. But not me. I was depressed, uncomfortable because I wasn't living on the edge. It wasn't that I was an adrenaline junkie. I was just comfortable living with risk. Now, I am not alone in this; many survivors of family and personal trauma follow the same path. But for most of my life, that was me.

In short, I was back living in Detroit, working on that factory line, a lost man with no future. I had recently endured being molested and had no idea where I was going. I was a mess.

I attempted to keep the Lord out of my life as much as possible. My memories of happier days following the Lord were relegated to the ash heap of memories seldom retrieved. Any hope was barely hanging on, and it showed in every aspect of my life.

Transmission Job

Not long after my close call at Vernors, I took a job at a transmission shop run by my brother Bob at Gratiot and 6 Mile Roads. For those who know the city of Detroit, south of 8 Mile Road is a no-go zone. From the decrepit and abandoned buildings to the criminal atmosphere, it is clear that the risk of venturing into these parts of the city is a real and present danger. My brother was the manager, and I became the assistant manager. Sure, I was still in Detroit and in a gang-infested area, but it was great to bond with Bob again.

During the period that I worked there, we had times where guys showed up with baseball bats because we sold their car that they never picked up or they thought we ripped them off. My brother carried a gun in his back pocket so that if anyone were to shoot me, he would shoot them. Because of this, I felt sort of safe—that is, until something happened with a local gang member who had been our customer.

Here's how it went down: the gang member brought his car in for a transmission diagnosis. Normally, we would charge seventy-five dollars to remove the damaged transmission from the car, after which we'd call to tell them what the damage was and how much it would cost to rebuild the transmission. This time, we erred, and before I got the customer's approval, the mechanics had rebuilt and replaced his transmission—which did need replacing. His car now had a good transmission, but when he showed up at the shop to see that the transmission was in his car and not on a bench, he thought that his old transmission had been fine and that we were just trying to rip him off.

Yes, we screwed up, but we weren't trying to cheat him. The gang guy left the shop and returned later with a couple more thugs. We were filled with dread and panic coiling in our chests; this was the very scenario we were most afraid of happening. Sure, we had close calls before with plenty of threats thrown our way. But we were street-smart enough to know that if a person ever intended to actually harm us, they wouldn't threaten us first. It was clear this was a serious threat, so we rushed to the phone to call the police for help.

THE END OF DETROIT; THE START OF MY LIFE

The cops actually showed up, but right after I got into the customer's car to show them that it was working well. The cops took off, leaving me alone with this gang of thugs who basically kidnapped me and took me for a ride. Being astute to the unwritten rules of what happens when you cheat those who rule the streets, I knew the outcome–I was not going to live through this.

After a twenty-minute ride around town, where they showed their guns to me and threatened me, they finally dumped me off somewhere in Detroit–I had no idea where. I couldn't believe it; I was still alive. At the time, I was a smoker, and right then, I needed a cigarette as well as to figure out where I was. My hands were vibrating like a hummingbird's wings, making it impossible to steady them enough to flick my lighter and spark the flame that would light my cigarette. I stopped a stranger to ask them where I was and to light my cigarette. I then found a payphone and called my brother to come pick me up.

There I was, flirting with danger once again. I was still working in a dangerous area at a place where we had to regularly pay off the police for protection. Every couple of months, the cops would come around with tickets to the Policeman's Ball, and we'd be obligated to buy a couple hundred dollars' worth, always in cash. To this day, I am not sure if there ever was an actual ball or if it was just a way for the cops to shake us down for money. As soon as the cops would leave, we always threw the tickets in the trash.

We handled most dangerous situations ourselves and only called the cops if the matter was truly life or death. In fact, that neighborhood was so rough that many times, we'd show up in the morning only to find that our guard dog was dead and stuff was stolen from our yard. At those times, we wouldn't bother to call the police. We'd just replace the lost goods and get another guard dog. It was all part of doing business.

During the whole time I worked at the transmission shop, six months was the longest that any of our guard dogs stayed alive. That shop wasn't a good place for me, but it was much worse to be a guard dog.

Time to Go

By this point in my life, I was done with Detroit. I knew that I had to make a change, and I knew that the chaos that always seemed to follow me would eventually be the end of me. Moving out of Detroit was a no-brainer.

I heard from Bob that the transmission shop owner had stores in Tampa Bay and Corpus Christi that needed management help, so I jumped at the opportunity. I flipped a coin to make the choice: heads for Texas, tails for Florida. I got tails. I soon packed up all I owned, and off to Tampa Bay, I went, not knowing a soul there or what was ahead. It was another opportunity for a fresh start away from the horrors of Detroit and my childhood. Looking back, it was the right way to go. God was looking out for me on that coin flip.

God was definitely looking out for me because, thanks to that move to Tampa Bay, my life was about to drastically change for the better: relationally, spiritually, and emotionally. Thanks to that move, I would providentially find the key to freedom—freedom found in forgiveness.

Wisdom and Insight from This Chapter

Based on my experience, I can tell you that allowing the wound of unforgiveness to exist leads to a patchwork of broken emotions and feelings that will take much time and effort to unpack and repair later. It is much wiser to take the time to confront and address the issue as early as possible to avoid a much larger wound down the line. It's been said that it is better to have a fence at the top of a cliff than an ambulance at the bottom.

My life has taught me that the earlier you tackle the pain of unforgiveness, the fewer repairs there will be to make in the long run. It is astounding how the scars of emotional trauma can rise up and manifest in a myriad of ways. Its presence looms over us from the shadows, creeping into our thoughts and dictating our emotional responses like a puppeteer pulling strings.

The journey continues . . .

CHAPTER 8

Key Turning Point #3— Unusual Path to Forgiving

> Getting over a painful experience is much like crossing monkey bars. You have to let go at some point in order to move forward.
>
> —**Chicken Soup for the Soul: Think Possible** [11]

Once in Florida, I was safe from the abuse and danger I had left behind in Detroit. They say you can't run from your problems, but sometimes, the smartest choice is to just move. This was the case with me. Because I was in a new city, I was able to make a fresh start.

I got an apartment and had a roommate who was a one-legged, gay, recovering alcoholic (you just can't make this stuff up!). For fun, I would often go into his room in the morning, grab his prosthesis, and tease him by telling him to get himself together. He was a great roommate, and despite his own issues, he was happy and helped me have a more positive outlook on life. He shared with me, "What you believe is wrong with you is exactly what makes you unique and loved." With all his issues, here he was encouraging me with an overwhelming acceptance, and celebration, of my imperfections.

After moving to Tampa, I attempted to continue in the transmission business—it's what had enabled me to move down there in the first place—but I hated it. It carried too many bad memories for me, with even more to come, so I decided to try selling residential real estate. Real estate utilized my sales skills as well as my love of working for myself.

Discovery of "Why Forgiveness?" —Brian Tracy

Then, it happened. I was invited by a business associate to attend a Brian Tracy seminar called "The Psychology of Achievement" to help improve my work performance and build my career. I had no idea that what was about to happen would so drastically change the trajectory of my world for the positive and be the foundation for my transition to forgiveness.

During the seminar, I sat in a room with around twenty or so others while we watched Brian Tracy speak on a TV as a facilitator helped us along with our workbooks so we could learn these new concepts.

It helped my business, but even more, it transformed the rest of my world as I knew it. What was done to my brothers and me was bad, really bad. However, here Brian Tracy was telling me that:

To be responsible = Control, freedom, and positive emotions.

To be irresponsible = A lack of control and freedom, plus negative emotions and excuses.

Further, he went on to teach me that I was always free to *choose* the quality of my emotional life.

What a concept! I have a choice? I can be free from the pain, shame, and blame? The major obstacle to my freedom was my negative emotions, but here he was, permitting me to be free of the anger and resentment toward the people and events in my life that had caused me so much pain.

KEY TURNING POINT #3—UNUSUAL PATH TO FORGIVING

He said, "There is a direct relationship between your acceptance of the personal responsibility for your emotional well-being and the elimination of your negative feelings."

Although it was a recorded presentation on the TV, it seemed like Brian Tracy was speaking directly to me when he said, "If it's to be, it's up to *me!*" Somehow, I thought of this as, "If I choose to forgive, it won't change my past, but it will change my future!"

His words were so radical that I mentally began to fight them. I kept thinking, *Don't you know what happened to me? I have every right to be full of blame. How can you tell me that I'm responsible when I was young and innocent?*

He then went on to share that blame looks to the past rather than the future and that the key to ridding yourself of negative emotions is to eliminate *blame*, which consists of 99 percent of negative emotions. Essentially, he was telling me to eliminate blame and negative emotions with the following affirmation:

"I am responsible."

He shared that even though it may not feel like it, I am the one who *controls* my future. If I want to be free from pain, I must accept complete responsibility from this moment forward. He further taught me that everything I am to be and every emotion I feel is *my choice*. Rather than blame my past, I could be responsible for my well-being on every level if I am willing to take that responsibility. And if I did that, I would gain hope, understanding, and freedom.

Wow.

Up to that point in my life, I had seen myself only as a victim and had thus justified all my actions and blamed all my problems on my dad.

Yes, I was who I was mainly because of what happened to me. But if I wanted to achieve true, full freedom, I needed to take responsibility for my emotional well-being and stop blaming my parents or the abuse that my brothers and I endured for so long. Most importantly, I could no longer *justify* my actions by blaming my offenders or offenses against me.

The training opened the door to a realm of understanding that had been previously inaccessible to me. The anger of the past suddenly dissipated, and a glorious epiphany illuminated my thoughts. Blame always looks *at the past*, at what cannot be changed. Responsibility always looks to the *future*.

As Brian Tracy taught me, "The question of the responsible person is *what can we do from here?*" and when I asked that question of myself, I began to feel in control, and equally as important, I was on my way to feeling worthy once again.

So, I made a pact with myself that when I felt the negative feelings creeping back in, I would say to myself, "If it's to be, it's up to me!" I would do this to be free of the chains of my past and give myself back control of my emotions and my happiness.

I bought Brian Tracy's cassette tape series called *The Psychology of Achievement*, and I replayed this one section in cassette three so much that I wore out the tape. Little did I know that with Brian Tracy's help, I had unlocked the secret to real and lasting forgiveness and was on my way to a new life.

For too long, I had avoided confronting the realities of my life by either blaming others or not taking full responsibility for who I was and what I had become. From Brian Tracy, I learned that I couldn't blame everything that had happened to me on others. From that moment on, I resolved to choose the quality of my emotional life and, by extension, the rest of my life.

Instead of finding someone to blame, I began to take responsibility. The next thing I knew, Tracy's ideas were changing my life; it was truly

KEY TURNING POINT #3—UNUSUAL PATH TO FORGIVING

the beginning of my path to forgiveness. That seminar got me started on this life-changing path, and I applied his words of wisdom to my life. I was no longer lost and alone; I had found support and guidance, and my life was finally on the path to transformation.

More importantly, I truly forgave my dad for who he was and all he did. Removing that backpack of anger, resentment, and pain made me a free man for the first time in my life. And it felt great!

Dad Sobers Up

And then it happened, I finally got the call. Mom said that both she and my dad had sobered up. Mom had checked herself into rehab, and Dad was going to Alcoholics Anonymous, and they had turned their lives over to the Lord. The words I heard felt like a jolt to my core. I felt like I had been transported to a whole new realm, one of possibility. I had to pinch myself to make sure I wasn't dreaming. *Is this really happening? Could change finally be within reach?*

Oh, and there was one more thing she wanted to tell me: they were moving to Florida just outside of Orlando and not far from where I lived, to be exact. And if that news wasn't strange enough, I found out that they would be moving to a clothing-optional community there. It was strange to think that my now sober and Bible-believing parents were going to live in a nudist community, but hey, at least they were finally on the right track.

Over the next several years, I started spending time with my dad. I went with him and my mother to at least a hundred AA meetings. My dad and I even joined a bowling league together, and I was actually enjoying spending time with him. Although at this point, I had already forgiven him, we learned together what reconciliation looked like. My dad, the man who should have gone to jail for the rest of his life for the horrendous things he did to our family, was now sober and had given his life to the Lord. He was truly a changed man. It would have been wonderful if my brothers had been willing to forgive and get to know this new man.

Years later, while I was watching TV one night with Dad, out of the blue, he said to me, "Mark, if there is anything I did to you when you were younger, I'm sorry." It was the wimpiest apology I had ever heard, especially given all that he had done. And yet, I immediately responded, in truth, that I had already forgiven him. As soon as I had uttered those words, we went back to watching TV as if nothing major had happened. It wasn't until the next day that I thought about what he had said and how crazy it was. I knew then—and still know now—that I did not need an apology from my father to forgive him. I just needed to forgive him, which I had already done prior to his change of heart and long before he apologized. Thanks to what I had learned from Brian Tracy and my own decision to forgive my dad, I was well on my way to understanding and living what forgiveness is and isn't. I am the one who benefitted the most by forgiving a good man.

God Winked at Me

Earlier, when I lived in Detroit, one of my roommates stole $600 from me and left without notice in the middle of the night. I figured I'd never get that money back, so I moved on and more or less forgot about it.

Well, one night, Dad didn't feel like going to their AA meeting, and Mom called to see if I could go in his place, so I did. It was a small meeting in a little town in the middle of Florida outside of Orlando—with only twenty or so people in attendance. Lo and behold, among them was that former roommate who had moved there all the way from Detroit, where he had ripped me off. He was at the AA meeting because he was a recovering alcoholic. He even paid me back $200 of the $600.

Even though I never saw or heard from him again, the entire experience was as if I had gotten a little wink from God as if to say, "Hey, I know you're there—I haven't forgotten you." Because running into that guy over a thousand miles away in a small-town AA meeting was a statistically mind-boggling occurrence.

Marriage and a Baby Girl

I was smitten the moment I saw a beautiful woman at a meeting. "Hi, I'm Mark, and I'd love to take you out." She invited us—my one-legged, gay, recovering alcoholic roommate and me—over for dinner at her house with her parents. Our nerves were on edge as we rang the doorbell, but I managed to remind my friend to wipe his feet, then followed with "I mean wipe your *foot*," and we both had a good laugh. The smell of freshly cooked Cuban food wafted through the house as the family gathered around the dinner table, laughing and smiling warmly. Every bite of the sumptuous meal was perfectly seasoned, and there was authentic love in the family, providing a comforting atmosphere. In that moment, I may have fallen in love with her family before falling in love with the woman who would become my wife.

That was the start of our two-year romance, which evolved into our getting married and having a beautiful daughter. My precious little daughter was perfect in every way. As I stepped onto the path of creating the family of my dreams, I once again felt a wave of optimism wash over me. I remembered back to my childhood days, lounging in the backyard, watching the planes soar overhead in the expansive sky, and feeling a sense of awe and anticipation. Now, I felt that same thrill of possibility, and I allowed myself to revel in the knowledge that I was finally on the brink of achieving my dreams of a real family.

And all this, especially my mom and dad's transformation and God's wink, came just in time for me to really use my newfound lesson in forgiveness in a way that I didn't see coming.

And so it was that early in the morning, around 4:30 a.m. on January 3, 1986, that I got a call from my brother Bob that would shake my world and test everything I thought I knew about forgiving and forgiveness.

Wisdom and Insight from This Chapter

Through the combination of hard work, the Lord's blessing, Brian Tracy's lessons, and these principles of forgiveness, I was able to achieve success. This achievement allowed me to be invited to the palace in the United Arab Emirates, where I had the privilege of dining with His Highness and His Excellency. Yes, I've dined from dumpsters and dined with kings and everything in between.

From my dad's transformation, I learned that you are never too old or have done too much evil to find God's grace, redemption, and forgiveness.

Regarding victim mentality, we have legitimate reasons for always being a victim. Each and every victim has the right to haul around their own backpacks filled with pain, shame, and blame.

I get it.

However, each victim must also remember that:

- Victims are *powerless.*
- Victims have no control over their lives.

- Victims are at the mercy of others and are passengers in the game of life.
- Victims can only react.
- Victims are prisoners.
- A victim has an excuse, and with that excuse, they can justify any kind of behavior.

Because of what happened to you, your victimhood allows you to justify your negative emotions. You can then excuse being the way you are because of what happened to you. But when you take responsibility for your emotional well-being, you eliminate blame and replace it with responsibility.

However, when we blame and feel guilty, we feel worthless, and these feelings take the form of the thought or attitude that *I'm not enough*. Those who have spent a long time in an environment of destructive criticism and lack of love are plagued by *self-hatred* and *self-condemnation*.

I understand that most people would rather *fight* to stay in pain than surrender and be healed. But taking responsibility for what happens now provides peace and freedom.

The journey continues . . .

CHAPTER 9

Each Brother Takes a Different Path

> Blame is simply the discharging of discomfort and pain.
> It has an inverse relationship with accountability.
> —**Brené Brown** [12]

As I've mentioned before, my brothers took a lot more abuse than I did while we were growing up. But instead of dealing with that abuse and processing how it affected them, they all swept it under the rug, which I suppose is the typical way of dealing with trauma. Of course, you can't experience the level of trauma they did, refuse to deal with it, and not suffer some consequences down the road, which is what happened with each of my brothers.

BOB

On January 3, 1986, at 4:30 a.m., my brother Bob called me. Even at that unusual time to call and wake me out of a good night's sleep, it was still great to hear from him. As soon as he started talking, I thought he was drunk because his speech was slurred. He told me that he called to say how much he loved me and that he was so sorry for everything that had happened and for who he was. I told him that I loved him and that we were okay. At that moment, I didn't suspect anything big was up.

In my mind, it was just a drunk phone call from my brother Bob. After talking for a few minutes, he said he had to go, so we hung up. I drifted off to sleep with a smile on my face, still basking in the warmth of my brother's ramblings, even though he was clearly under the influence of some kind of intoxicating substance.

About ninety minutes later, my phone rang again. But this time, it wasn't Bob. It was a police officer. His message was short but devastating: my brother Bob had taken his own life by starting up five cars in the garage where he was working and letting the fumes take his life.

It wasn't until then that I realized that Bob was actually committing suicide while on the phone with me some ninety minutes before. He hadn't been drunk; no, his slurred speech was a sign of the hypoxia caused by his inhaling all that carbon monoxide.

I now had to confront a hard, cold reality: my brother, who had led me to the Lord, taught me business, taught me how to sell, and was the family member I was closest to on this planet, was now dead.

Before Bob decided to end his life, he was a mess. He was in trouble with the IRS, his marriage was in shambles, and of course, he had never even begun to deal with the abuse he had suffered as a child. He left behind a journal of his last few days along with a suicide note, which I still keep on my desk.

The note that he left behind read,

> I am sorry!!!! You don't have any idea how much I hate myself. I hated my father, and what am I? I'm sorry for what I'm doing, but it is the only way I can show you how bad I feel. God I am sorry! I am nothing. Please take the best care of our children. I love them so. I'm sleepy now.

Suicide is brutal on everyone it touches, but Bob's suicide solved nothing. His suicide, like all suicides, didn't take away the pain; it just passed it on to those left behind.

Bob's loved ones were now left to clean up the mess. He left behind a wife and two children aged four and seven.

After a Suicide

After a suicide, those who remain behind are left with "shoulda," "coulda," and "woulda." Surviving relatives, friends, and loved ones can't help but replay every conversation they had with the deceased during the last months of their loved one's life. They wonder if they *shoulda* picked up on the signals of distress, and if they *coulda* done something more, something different, they *woulda*. If those feelings of shoulda, coulda, woulda are allowed to continue, the resulting guilt and shame often tears apart the lives of those left behind.

Bob chose to end his life, and yet when I spoke to him that last time, I had reasonably assumed that he was just a little drunk. Despite my closeness to him, I had no way of knowing what was really going on with him. For quite a period of time, I struggled with those feelings before realizing that given the information I had to work with, I had handled that phone call at 4:30 a.m. from an intoxicated loved one in the only way I woulda expected of me. Regardless of my sound reasoning for not carrying the responsibility of handling the situation differently, it still hurts to this day.

But it wasn't only Bob whom I had to forgive. After he died, I found myself angry at God to the point that I was pointing up in heaven, giving God the finger, as it were. I kept asking myself, *How could a good God let this happen?* I took my pain and shame and blamed it on God rather than on my parents or my brother himself.

After much contemplation and understanding of both forgiveness and blame, I accepted that God had not caused Bob to take his own life; it was Bob's own free will. Simply put, I not only had to forgive my brother for what he had done, but I also had to stop blaming God for allowing him to do it—at least that's how I felt.

I take great inspiration from the words of Brené Brown, whom I quoted at the start of this section: "Blame is simply the discharging of discomfort and pain." My blame was a manifestation of my anger.

I still miss Bob every day. There's so much of my life now that I would love to share with him. I look forward to seeing him in heaven someday, and when I do see him, the first thing I'll do is punch him in the jaw for being so selfish, followed by giving him the biggest hug he's ever received.

Our tendency to blame God and others for our troubles can infect all our relationships. In my case, it took me years to work through these feelings of shame and anger. I hope you never experience a loved one taking their own life, but if you have, you know how suicide can cause immense grief and sorrow for those who remain. It is a final choice to what may be a temporary problem. Unforgiveness can have any number of detrimental impacts, including suicide and divorce.

Unforgiveness Takes a Toll on My Marriage

My wife, an incredible woman and great mother to our daughter, had issues that would cause her to lash out in anger at seemingly small things. Had I been better equipped to handle such sudden outbursts, the resulting divide in our marriage could have been avoided.

When she married me, she believed that I would change one day. When I married her, I believed she would never change. We both were mistaken.

I had a bad case of the "butchus." You know what that is. When she would get upset about something I didn't do or I did wrong, I would shamefully respond, "Butchu didn't do that other thing either." Rather than dealing with my own feelings of being a victim, I deflected the blame back on her. This case of the butchus is never good in a marriage, and in our case, it ended up in many unsettled arguments that were unnecessary.

My ability to cope with such emotions from my childhood, Bob's suicide, and my shame from the sexual abuse were unresolved at this point. The buildup of unresolved conflict eventually resulted in 2003 with an amicable yet heartbreaking divorce that affected our entire family. I wish I could tell my younger self how freeing it is to forgive and take full account of my responsibilities for change and how doing so dramatically improves relationships. This unforgiveness, coupled with shame and feelings of being unworthy, caused a ripple effect in all aspects of my life, especially evident in my most precious relationships.

JIM

The following story illustrates the kind of person Jim had become because of Dad's abuse coupled with his wound of unforgiveness.

Back when I still lived in Detroit and not long after I had returned from California, Jim called me one day. By this time, he was married with a daughter and had been living in a town just north of Boston. On the call, he told me that he had just landed a job in Detroit and was moving back to the area.

"Can you help me move back?" he asked.

Now, I don't know anyone who *likes* to help others move, regardless of whether the person needing help is friend or family. Moving is a tough chore, and moving across states is even worse. Despite all this, I said sure.

"You just need to fly me there, and I can do it," I said.

On the first night after a day of packing and moving furniture, I was sitting in his living room watching TV with him, just relaxing for a bit, when something odd happened.

Suddenly, he yelled to his wife Gail (who had been upstairs) to come back downstairs.

"Gail! Turn the channel!" he screamed.

Without a word, she hurried down the stairs to where we were and turned the channel on the TV set (this was before all TV sets had remote controls). After she changed the channel, she dutifully stood next to the TV and waited to see if he approved of the change, and when he said okay, she went back upstairs to resume whatever she had been doing, probably more packing.

Obviously, this was some sort of bizarre routine of theirs, but even if she was agreeing to it, it was still abominable. My brother had legs and was completely capable of changing his own damn channel. I was mad, but I held my temper. Instead, I told him, "Hey, the next time you need to change the channel, just let me know—*I'll* do it."

The next day, while Jim and I were talking in the kitchen, he yelled to his teenage daughter Tanya to come into the kitchen. I was transfixed on her as she stood at attention in front of the fridge for what seemed like eternity. Finally, Jim went to get something out of the fridge and yelled at her for being in the way, apparently unaware or having forgotten why he had called her there in the first place. No longer being needed by her dad, she left the kitchen without saying a word.

At that point, I said, "That's it. I've had enough. You're out of control. You're incredibly abusive."

As we got started on our journey, I angrily told him I was done helping him; he was on his own. From this point on, I was nothing but a passenger getting a ride back to Detroit. I couldn't bring myself to assist someone who was so vitriolic in their treatment of others, spewing out harsh and hurtful words with every breath. In a great way, I was suddenly transported back to my childhood, a spark of recognition igniting within me. Jim's gestures and mannerisms were so uncannily reminiscent of our dad, the same man he had so vehemently detested and reviled. I could almost see our father's face in Jim's, and the similarities were almost too much to fathom.

We barely got started on the ride back when he asked me to help him with the trailer hitch towing their car behind the U-Haul. I snapped back at him, my voice rising with frustration, reminding him that I was no longer helping; I was nothing more than a rider along for the ride. Suddenly, we were in an argument, with words flying back and forth, each of us louder than the last. The verbal arguing ended up turning into a physical fight, wrestling mostly, and during the fracas, he broke the necklace I was wearing. At this point, I was determined not to continue riding up front with him but planned instead to sit on a couch in the back of the U-Haul with the trailer door cracked. I was setting things up inside the U-Haul when Jim suddenly came up from behind, slammed the door shut, and locked me in.

The U-Haul felt like a prison as we drove from Boston to Michigan. I was trapped for over thirteen hours, sealed in a stuffy, cramped compartment with no way out. Desperate for some fresh air, I thankfully had a razor with me so I could slice through the weather stripping and let some fresh air into the stuffy trailer.

When we came to a stop outside of Detroit, I started kicking at the door from the inside and yelling, angry that he had trapped me in there. But instead of his voice, I heard his wife's. She let me out, but Jim was nowhere to be found.

After over thirteen hours of being locked in that U-Haul, I was now like a wild animal. Gail told me that Jim wasn't going to come back until I calmed down. After getting a chance to relieve myself in the rest stop and searching everywhere I could to take revenge on Jim, I finally calmed down. Jim returned from wherever he was hiding out, but instead of taking me home, he drove me to the outskirts of town and let me out. I had to take a cab to get back home, but at least I was now out of that blasted U-Haul trailer.

At the time, Jim owned a pair of shoes that he paid $400 for, and while I had been in the U-Haul, I noticed them with the intent of plotting my payback on him. I wanted to hit him where it hurt, so I stole one of his shoes, not both, but rather just one, knowing that he would eventually notice its absence.

The next morning, he called.

"Where's my shoe?" he said.

"Where's my necklace?" I shot back. I then told him that if he paid me for what he had broken, I would give him his shoe back—we'd have an exchange.

Soon after, he showed up at our house. I was ready for him, shooting hoops in the back with a swagger of total dominance and swishing the basketball through the net with a satisfying thunk. My every movement was calm and collected, the attitude and posture of someone who believes they have the upper hand in the situation. I felt alive, in control, and triumphant.

"Where is my fifteen dollars for my necklace?" I asked.

Instead of exchanging, Jim demanded his shoe. Suddenly, he reached into the garage and pulled out a bat and started to drag me to the house. The power dynamic had shifted, and he now held me firmly in his grasp with the bat waving over my head. His eyes were like ice, seizing control of the situation and leaving me powerless in his wake. I was now at his mercy.

I was able to break away from him and ran to jump the backyard fence—I could do that back then. Because he was older and, by then, quite overweight, Jim couldn't make the jump. However, the grass that I was about to launch over the fence was wet, so I slipped and fell, and this gave him enough time to reach me. With a terrorizing face just like that from Jack Nicolson in the movie *The Shining*, he reared back and was about to hit me with the bat. He was full of anger and was going for a big hit, only in this case, my head was the baseball. Just as he swung the bat with the intensity and determination of Hank Aaron going for his 756th home run, I stuck my foot up in the way, and his bat hit my foot instead of my head. My move spared my head, but boy did it hurt my foot and ankle.

Jim dragged me to the back door as I limped along the way, but I then tried to block him out. As he struggled to get in through the partially opened door, I punched him as hard as I could, right in the eye. As he forcefully shoved the door in an attempt to reach me, I let go of it, and he toppled inside, face-planting dramatically onto the floor with a loud thud. At that moment, I bolted out the door and ran out into the street. A car was coming by, and I jumped right into their path, waving my arms. They were going to either stop or they were going to hit me. Fortunately, the car stopped, and I said to them, "You have to let me in; there's a man coming after me with a bat." Fortunately for me, they did, and they then drove me to the ER so I could get my foot looked at. Luckily, it wasn't broken.

Now, every time I see a U-Haul, I think of that experience.

Years later, whenever Jim would ask a favor or suggest some sort of activity, I would always reply, "Well, I'm fine with it as long as it doesn't include a U-Haul." And we would always laugh. With my brothers, what would be considered outrageous in other families was a source of amusement. We would revel in the absurdity of it.

Because of the abuse he had suffered, Jim was lost in his anger. Of all of us, Jim took the most physical abuse. Later, Jim went on to emotionally abuse his wife and daughter.

Some might have a hard time forgiving someone who had locked them up for thirteen-plus hours in a U-Haul, but I have forgiven my brother.

To me, it was clear that Jim blamed everything bad that happened to him and in his life on Dad. If one were to assign some blame, Jim was who he was largely because of Dad. And yet Jim—like all of us—still had a choice. Forgiving Dad would have meant that Jim was now responsible for whatever was going on, or not going on, in his life. Blaming someone else for your problems means that you aren't responsible and that you have no control. Blaming someone else makes you a victim. That blame essentially becomes a security blanket that too many people hang on to, allowing them to shrink from addressing their own actions and choices. Letting go of that blanket of blame would mean that they are now responsible for their life, and that was something that Jim (and many like him) apparently couldn't face.

After Bob's suicide, Jim was angry that Bob had taken his life, but he was also angry that Bob hadn't called him like Bob had called me. To his dying day, Jim struggled with the coulda, shoulda, woulda concerning

Bob's death. Jim and Bob were close as kids, even though they got into some really nasty fights, and Bob's suicide cut Jim deeply.

Jim always struggled with me because I was not angry and resentful against Mom and Dad like he was. Jim told me that I lived in denial; I told him that I was practicing forgiveness. "I'm sorry, but I'm not going to be eaten up with anger," I told him. I also told him that he had every right to stay angry, but if he wanted to find freedom, he would have to forgive.

And yes, unforgiveness will cause health problems (how could it not?), which is what I believe happened with Jim. He died of cancer at around age seventy-two. At one point, he weighed well over four hundred pounds, which got a little better after he had intestinal bypass surgery. Jim also smoked a couple of packs of cigarettes a day. He didn't expect to live a long life, and because of his actions and attitudes, he didn't. He passed away still full of anger and resentment from what happened to him during childhood.

Relational Credit Score

Years before Jim passed away, I set boundaries with him. You see, I had forgiven Jim, but I wasn't ready to trust him. Remember, forgiving someone who has hurt or abused us does not mean we must reconcile with them, trust them, or again become close to them, regardless of the kind of abuse. Thus, forgiving Jim did not mean that I had to be subjected to further abuse from him. Yes, I was able to forgive him, but I also knew that it was healthy and wise to keep my distance from him to prevent him from continuing to hurt me.

During Jim's last years, I heard from family members that he had begun to change for the better. At that point, I considered reaching out to him. But when I then learned that he had recently told his own daughter to "f— off," I decided to wait to contact him and kept those boundaries intact.

This brings up an important point that I've learned regarding forgiveness and reconciliation. Sometimes, the offender we've forgiven does make changes for the better. But does that mean that we should immediately begin to trust them?

I see this often with drug and alcohol abusers who have sobered up after doing years and even decades of damage to their relationships with their friends and family. Another example of this is when someone has committed infidelity, which does deep damage to the relationship. After getting clean or making an honest change for the good, the offending parties in these situations often expect those around them to immediately trust them once again. And yet, trusting someone as before isn't always possible or wise.

I believe that we all develop or carry what I like to call our *Relational Credit Score*, which, much like a financial credit score, is a measurement of the level of trust between two people. Even though we can forgive and the offender can change or at least stop their bad behaviors, our *Relational Credit Score* has taken a beating and may take years or decades to be repaired. For the loved ones of substance abusers, this may mean finding ways to track their comings and goings and know they are on the straight and narrow. And for those whose partner has cheated, it may also mean more accountability by keeping a closer eye on their whereabouts—like putting a tracker on their phone—for a time.

Again, while forgiveness is truly miraculous and means that our debt has indeed been forgiven and written off, our *Relational Credit Score* is not what it was before, and it will take time for others to again trust us fully—if ever.

As I wrote off the debt with Jim by forgiving him, I took account of his *Relational Credit Score* and saw that it was too low for true reconciliation between us. To protect myself from further hurt, I had to keep some distance between us. Reconciliation takes both sides to strive for the better, and since Jim passed away, I was left with that question of what could have been if he had stayed around for us to mend our broken relationship.

MIKE

Mike's existence is a fragile one, buffeted by schizophrenia's relentless hold on him. He struggles to cope with its daily challenges, a valiant effort to simply stay afloat in a sea of vivid memories of the past. He lives a simple but safe life now, spent mostly in his own world, a place where he tries to escape the haunting memories of the abuse he suffered. Mike currently lives on disability income in a special complex in Florida for the mentally challenged.

Like many victims of child abuse, Mike can barely sleep at night because of nightmares that take him back to age twelve, when he received his worst abuse from our dad. Mike is one of the nicest guys you could ever meet, but he can't deal with the real world. I wake up, almost daily, to find a bunch of rambling emails from Mike that he has typed the previous night. I love hearing from him, and I've saved dozens that relate to the stories of our family.

For most of his life, Mike refused to refer to our parents as Mom and Dad, choosing instead to refer to them by their first names, Earl and Shirley. Only in the last couple of years, as he's learned about forgiving, he has started saying that he now looks forward to a heavenly reunion with those in our family who have already passed on.

Even someone as wounded as Mike can come to realize that anything is forgivable.

Like many who are abused, Mike continued the cycle of abuse. While Mike was still a teenager, he sexually abused Jim's daughter. He is the living example of the adage I keep repeating that hurt people hurt people.

Years ago, I gave Mike a car, but he has such a big heart that he soon gave that car away to someone he thought needed it more. As a result, he rode his bike to get around. Mike was careening recklessly down the street on his bicycle when he suddenly ran a stop sign and was struck by a car. A witness to the crash described it as so violent that Mike's skull was split open, and his brain was visible through the wreckage of his crushed head. He was rushed to the hospital and remained there for the next six months as he underwent a seemingly endless series of surgeries and rehab. After his release, Mike stayed at our home for a while before finally settling back into his apartment.

For a short time, we helped Mike get on medication to treat his schizophrenia, but dealing with the real world proved too much for him; it was just easier for him to live in his imaginary world. As a result, we decided that the best option for Mike, at this point at least, was for him to discontinue the medication.

Mike is still alive and is starting to forgive, but his life isn't one any of us would want in place of our own.

Summing Up

In my family, there were four boys, all raised under the same chaotic, abusive roof. But as we aged, we each chose different paths:

- One stayed angry and died too soon.
- One took his own life.
- One now lives in an imaginary world, mostly out of touch with reality.
- One chose to forgive and be happy.

Life has undoubtedly thrown hardships at you, but after your suffering, what path have you taken? What path will you continue to take? Will you choose to stay angry, check out of life early, check out mentally, or will you choose to move forward and experience some of the joy that life still has to offer?

Some people escape through drugs, alcohol, sex, or abusing others; all are traps made possible by the choice of unforgiveness. And just like a physical wound, emotional wounds left unhealed infect you. But instead of infecting your body, they infect your soul with new problems. And you have to own those problems because you did not treat that wound. Until you begin to heal those wounds by forgiving, you won't be free.

The wound of unforgiveness can infect everything, especially those you love the most.

I'm not going to kid you. My path of forgiveness has been tough—really tough—but it was worth it. It's the only path that leads to life and happiness for those who have suffered wrongs. We four brothers took four different paths, but only one of us has fully discovered the path to freedom, happiness, and life.

So, what is unforgivable?

Nothing.

Freedom awaits you, but you can only find that freedom through forgiveness.

Wisdom and Insight from This Chapter

Perhaps the weight of Bob's shame and anger had been too much for him. That anger and Bob's inability to forgive helped drive him to end his life. What I'm saying is that the wound of unforgiveness can affect and infect everything, including all your relationships or even the decision to escape life itself. Being unable to forgive isn't ever listed as an official cause of death, but clearly, the wound of unforgiveness affected my brother.

My understanding of forgiveness made me realize that I had to forgive my brother Bob for ending his life. I had reached the point in my journey of understanding forgiveness where I could put all I had learned into practice, delving into its depths with a newfound appreciation and respect.

Through our forgiveness nonprofit of 70x7.org, I've not only seen lives changed for the better with forgiveness, but I've also witnessed lives saved from suicide. My favorite is this one:

> I have thought and contemplated suicide for a long time. On the surface, it looks like I have a wonderful life, but I just have had some really bad times lately that people do not see, and I didn't want to go on. I came very close; that is, until I read your story. It said, "Suicide doesn't take away the pain; it just puts it on someone else." It really made me realize how much it would hurt my family. I'm going to work through these problems. I just thought you should know that today, you saved a life.

If you're hanging on to your own security blanket of blame, you have my deepest sympathy, but as long as you do, you'll never find your freedom. All my brothers refused to let go and made blaming our dad their world, and all of them—and their children—paid the price.

I often meet with people who would love to be free of the pain and forgive, but they can't let go because doing so would mean that they are responsible for their emotional well-being and can no longer blame their offender. Some of us would rather fight to stay in pain than surrender to be healed. For those who live around people like this, unforgiveness is like secondhand smoke. They don't think that the other person's anger and inability to forgive will hurt them and affect those around them, but it does.

The journey continues . . .

CHAPTER 10

Key Turning Point #4— Taking Off the Mask

Don't judge me by my past. I don't live there anymore.
—**Author Unknown** (13)

I made my way to Atlanta in spring 2003 to embark on a daring business venture. Little did I know that this opportunity would eventually launch me on a journey that would span the globe, introducing me to new cultures from Asia to the Middle East.

On a beautiful fall Atlanta day that same year, a friend called to meet up for a drink at my favorite bar restaurant and meet her cousin, who was visiting from out of town. We chatted, but the whole time I couldn't take my eyes off a beautiful woman sitting two tables away who was chatting away with another lady. I believed that she was oblivious to my existence, but after paying my bill and saying goodbye to my friend and her cousin, I was pleased to see her sitting alone. I approached her. "Hi, my name is Mark." I then asked her, "Your name is?" She said, "Laura." The best I could come up with was, "Well, I think you are beautiful, and I hope to see you here again." As I stepped out of the door of the restaurant, I felt a pang of regret from my awkward introduction, thinking that I had messed up my one opportunity to get to know her.

Four days later, I went back, and there she was! We closed that place down, talking late into the evening, and we haven't been apart since. In 2006, we were married. She is my rock and my guide, a steadfast woman devoted to her faith, her strength and stability being exactly what I needed. We became highly involved in church, each day bringing us closer to the Lord.

Early on in our marriage, I shared parts of my past struggles and my journey of forgiveness with her, but only as much as I felt was necessary. I still had an invisible barrier to protect myself from the judgment of others. If they were to see the true extent of my imperfections, they would surely see that the real me who appeared to have it together was a fraud, and they would be repelled. I felt like a chameleon, desperately trying to conceal my true identity behind a mask to stop the world from seeing the parts of me I disliked, unwilling to expose myself to judgment or ridicule.

I kept this emotional wall of shame and unworthiness between me and anyone who tried to get close, never allowing myself to experience the joy of a genuine connection.

In 2014, my whole life changed.

It all happened when I experienced what would become the fourth key turning point in my life.

At our church, my wife and I joined what they call a community small group. For those not familiar with them, these groups are made up of church members who share a common stage of life. These couples meet regularly to talk, study, and build a deeper connection with the Lord. The main goal of such community small groups is to gather together and, as we call it, do life together.

KEY TURNING POINT #4—TAKING OFF THE MASK

Over the first few meetings, one by one, everyone shares their story. This generally includes sharing with others details about family, a synopsis of our life, and how we came to join the group.

During our first meeting, the very first person in our group to share was completely transparent, exposing his very emotional life experience. He described his past in vivid detail, recounting every sensation with an intensity that made it feel as though I were there in the moment with him. *Wow*.

Transparency breeds transparency and, if allowed, gives permission for others to do the same.

For the next two weeks, I was consumed by his story. I spent every waking minute reflecting on my own story of abuse and its accompanying pain, shame, and blame. Prior to that meeting, I had woken up each day, reached over, and put on a mask that told the whole world that everything with me was "A-okay!" It wasn't. I had spent my entire life pretending to be okay. If you've experienced this, you know how exhausting it can be.

I knew that in two weeks, it was going to be my turn to tell my story. Would I give a short version that glossed over all of the important—but gritty—details, or would I finally come clean and share it all?

For those two weeks, I thought and prayed about little else.

Sure, by that point in my life, I had achieved decisional forgiveness of my family, and I had shared part of my family experiences; I had experienced some of the benefits of forgiveness and reconciliation. But my version of sharing only told part of the story at a high level, almost as a reporter would report the news. There was never sharing all of what happened, including my sexual abuse and, most importantly, how it affected me, including the shame and feelings of being unworthy.

The more I kept silent, the more my shame grew. Of course, our natural impulse is to hide our injuries and imperfections from others. It's perhaps a primal reaction, much like the hurt animal in a herd of prey that tries desperately to hide its injuries from others in the herd or from roaming predators.

It is only when we expose our shame to the light of day that we diminish its power over us. This phenomenon is not new, and many have commented on it.

The vast majority of abused people wear a mask; others speak of it as putting up emotional walls to cover their personal shame. They wear their mask because they are sure that if people knew who they really were, they wouldn't like them and accept them as they are.

That was me.

After thinking and praying, and more thinking and praying, it became clear. I was tired of pretending to be someone I wasn't. I had grown weary of trying to mask my true self in the presence of God and those closest to me, pretending I had an abundance of strength when, in reality, I felt I was lacking. Every ounce of energy drained from my body, leaving me feeling hollow and exhausted. I was desperate to be seen and accepted just as I was and to finally feel like I was enough even with my flaws and my past. I was finally ready to share my whole story with the group—everything—and to finally tear off that mask and reveal my feelings of unworthiness, that I was not enough.

Sure, my wife knew part of my story already, but what I had shared with her previously was akin to what a big corporate media representative or PR firm shares about something bad that has happened at the company: high-level facts and only enough info to keep nosy reporters at bay. I had shared stories of my childhood and that my dad was abusive, but that was about it. I had never shared the part that cut the deepest, especially the sexual abuse I had suffered and the effect it had on me.

So, I brought my wife into the kitchen and told her that there were events in my life, issues, and feelings that I hadn't ever shared, not with anyone—not even her. "You'd better sit down," I told her.

I then proceeded to share *everything*, including what happened, how I felt about it, and why I responded so poorly in certain circumstances. My mask finally came off. I held nothing back.

Not only did I reveal events in my family that I had kept under wraps, but I also shared with her the real shameful me and more. It all came pouring out. I shared how I wasn't always doing as well as I seemed to be. I also told her the reason behind my ridiculing our hometown was because I didn't feel worthy to live in such an affluent environment, why I didn't like her helping me out with things and preferred doing them on my own, and why I had so few good Christian male friends. The simple fact was I felt they were better than me. Like water that seeks its own level, I felt more comfortable spending time with other broken people like me.

It all came out, including why I didn't feel worthy before God or her.

I had been living a lie.

Finally tearing down the wall I hid behind and telling my wife everything that day wasn't easy, but it felt *great*.

Being authentic changed *all* my relationships for the better, and it changed how I felt about myself—as someone worthy of good things.

So, what was different this time? Hadn't I already forgiven all those people in my past? Shouldn't I have already felt completely free?

I had finally unlocked the last piece of the puzzle. I was still living in shame with a negative self-appraisal of how I saw myself. Even though I had made so much progress on my forgiveness journey, when I looked into the mirror, I saw damaged goods. The level of self-condemnation was evidenced by the depth of my shame.

Shame needs three things to exist:

- Unforgiveness
- Judgment
- Concealment (keeping the hurt in the dark and not sharing what happened)

Up to this point, I was still enduring all three of those. At the same time, I learned that to take those three away, shame *can't* survive.

I had forgiven my dad, but I had not forgiven myself. I was no longer holding judgment over my dad, but I was unrealistically judging myself. And when it came to concealment, I was hiding all of what happened and how I felt behind my wall or mask so as not to let anyone see the real me.

To be fully healed of shame, the biggest factor proved to be breaking the cycle of concealment.

I can personally identify with the line in John Lynch's book *The Cure*, where he shares a profound question regarding feeling worthy: "What if there was a place so safe that the worst of me could be known, and I would discover that I would not be loved less, but more in the telling of it?" [14]

Finally, I began to feel loved and worthy just as I am. I was enough! Even how I related to God and how I believed God saw me was new.

And so when the time came for us to attend that next small group meeting, and it was my turn to share, I shared everything. And I haven't stopped since. It feels great to be free from that shame mask, and I never want to put it back on again.

KEY TURNING POINT #4—TAKING OFF THE MASK

The resulting paradigm shift that I experienced was so powerful that for the next four months, I launched on a journey of discovery to understand every detail of what had really happened and how it affected me today.

And as I did so, my level of forgiveness and self-worth grew.

I started seeing a therapist and got baptized. I finally felt, not just thought, that God and others loved and accepted me just as I am. My new self-worth journey started me on a mission of discovery that included devouring every word of every book I could get my hands on related to abuse and forgiveness.

By taking off the mask of shame, I was willing to fully heal by talking about our childhood in our own family, first with my brother Mike and then with my mother. Mike and I were shocked to find out that our mother did not know about the sexual abuse of her boys by her husband, our father. Now in her mid-eighties in age, she was devastated—not only to realize how much her boys were hurt, but she was suddenly having to deal with her own blame of why she was not there to protect her boys.

I won't sugarcoat this, the resulting conversations with the three of us were tough, really tough. However, at the same time, it was just what we needed to heal and work toward forgiving, really forgiving, so we could be free from resentment and shame.

My mom started seeing a therapist to actively seek forgiveness of our dad, what happened, and forgiving herself. The combination of honest conversations and her therapy resulted in amazing results in her. When she did pass away a few years later, she was truly happy once again and at peace. In her, I got to experience the power and freedom found in being honest with the past and the resulting forgiveness. She set the example for me of the total remission of the faults of our past.

I learned that there were two higher levels of forgiveness I had just uncovered, and it's those other levels of forgiveness that I encourage you to pursue to truly be free.

THE THREE TYPES OF FORGIVENESS EXPLAINED

Based on my own experience, the clinical psychology teaching of Dr. Everett Worthington, and theologians, there are three types or levels of forgiveness:

- Decisional forgiveness
- Emotional forgiveness
- Spiritual forgiveness

The first type, *decisional forgiveness*, is what I had done years ago: mentally forgiving those who had hurt me. This forgiveness happens in your head. This type of forgiveness is the essential first step to total forgiveness.

To help you visualize it, let me use an illustration. It's as if you have a room in your house that is full of garbage. It's full of nasty things that happened to you that affect your physical, emotional, and spiritual well-being. You don't even want to enter that room, and just the thought of it drags you down. Finally, one day you've had enough, and you decide to clean out that room. Well, *decisional forgiveness* is a conscious decision to finally clean all the garbage out of that room. The removal of the trash alone is a great step in itself and should be applauded.

The effort to decide to do so is a necessary first step that signals your desire to be rid of the mess that you've been carrying around in your head. This kind of forgiveness is a decisional letting go of resentment

KEY TURNING POINT #4—TAKING OFF THE MASK

and bitterness and the need for vengeance. Awesome. However, this kind of forgiveness does not include the end of the emotional pain and hurt. Even more so, it often does not end the rumination of the offender and the offense.

The second type or level, *emotional forgiveness*, is what I experienced when I opened up and told my story to my wife, my small group, and others.

To fully experience *emotional forgiveness*, you must remove the guilt and shame. This is about *feeling*, not just thinking, about both the forgiveness of the offender and that you are a worthy person. The additional element needed is to gain empathy for your offender. As I said, hurt people hurt people. No matter what torturous ordeals my dad had endured, his behavior could never be justified. However, by having empathy for him, I can understand that his life's ordeals influenced the man he became.

After experiencing *emotional forgiveness*, whenever I play that old, familiar video tape in my head of my dad, I now can fully experience empathy for him and remember what good times we had together. With this type of forgiveness, I realize that although he committed horrible offenses, those were a byproduct of his pain.

This type of forgiveness doesn't just happen in your head. With *decisional forgiveness* alone, people often continue to ruminate on the offense and offender; they replay their pain and hurt over and over in their heads. Through *emotional forgiveness*, the negative emotions attached to those memories are replaced with empathy for the offender and a feeling that you are worthy of better. The ruminations about the offense and the offender can finally come to an end. It *feels* great.

To revisit the room analogy, it's as if you now painted that cleaned room, added nice furniture, and decorated it. It now *feels* good to be in the room.

With the third type or level, *spiritual forgiveness*, there is remission, not just forgiveness of the wrongs. Remission means that the offenses are eradicated with *complete* clemency for the offender. The offender begins again with a clean slate. Think of it this way: if someone has cancer and they go into remission, the cancer is now gone!

If you want to be *totally* free, remission is where you want to be.

As Christians, we are familiar with this level of forgiveness through the example of Jesus Christ dying on the cross for the remission of our sins—He made it as though our sins had never happened. There was no longer a debt to repay.

> For this is my blood of the New Testament, which is shed for many for the remission of sins.
> **—Matthew 26:28 (KJV)**

> Now where remission of these is, there is no more offering for sin.
> **—Hebrews 10:18 (KJV)**

Through *emotional forgiveness*, you fill the room back up with things that make you feel good about being there, and you stop ruminating over and over about the transgression. Through *spiritual forgiveness*, you are now able to throw a party in your room. You may even be willing to invite the offender and have a total reconciliation, provided the offender is no longer an actual threat. Through *spiritual forgiveness*, you issue your offender a complete and unconditional pardon.

KEY TURNING POINT #4—TAKING OFF THE MASK

Spiritual forgiveness is a lofty goal to be sure; however, I know that it is attainable in this life because I've experienced it. This is the pinnacle of freedom found in forgiveness.

As an example of *spiritual forgiveness*, I recall a story that a businessman shared with me. In 2007, while training for an upcoming triathlon, he was riding his bicycle on a trail outside of Atlanta when he noticed a bee had landed on his helmet. His immediate reaction was to hit his helmet to rid himself of the bee and avoid being stung. When he did so, his elbow jostled the handlebars, causing him to lose his balance and be thrown headfirst over the bike. The accident broke his neck, and he is now a quadriplegic. Is he angry with himself or with God because this happened? No. Instead, he gives thanks to God that he has been entrusted with an experience such as this. He feels fully cleansed of the injustice that had been done to him. *That* is *spiritual forgiveness*.

Prior to removing my mask, I had achieved *decisional forgiveness* only. By achieving both *emotional* and *spiritual forgiveness*, I've learned to transform my heart and thoughts, replacing the darkest of feelings with empathy and understanding. Even for my dad, who deserved total condemnation, my chest is filled with warmth, goodwill, and compassion that I never thought possible. My heart has grown through empathetic understanding, a forgiveness level that I never knew I could feel.

Most people understand *decisional forgiveness*. But *emotional forgiveness* extends far deeper. And of course, *spiritual forgiveness* extends beyond that.

Freedom through forgiveness takes work. It takes dedicated daily effort, but the reward is well worth it.

Imagine yourself walking up a descending escalator. If you do nothing, you will descend. Taking a few steps here and there may allow you to stay in place. However, if you consistently climb, you will ascend to the top. Your reward is freedom from all that pain, shame, and blame.

Is all the effort worthwhile to exercise all the work needed to realize your freedom? This photograph of my dad and me, not long before he passed away, illustrates the mental and emotional peace I gained through forgiveness and reconciliation, a powerful sense that any offense can be healed.

So, I ask again, what is unforgivable? Nothing.

KEY TURNING POINT #4—TAKING OFF THE MASK

WISDOM AND INSIGHT FROM THIS CHAPTER

The author John Lynch asks what happens to us when we believe we're not enough?" [15]

- Those closest to you pay the most.
- You are uber-sensitive to even falsely perceived slights.
- You spend your days attempting to prove you're enough instead of simply living with nothing to prove.
- The real you never becomes fully known by anyone.
- You are distrustful of any affirmation.
- You isolate because it's very hard to stay in public, believing others can tell you're not enough.
- You hide your struggles, addictions, and failures.

As strange as this may sound to anyone who has not yet discovered emotional and spiritual forgiveness, I thank the Lord for all that pain. Today, I can say both that I was abused *and* am thankful for the journey I've been on—all in the same sentence. And I owe it all to taking off the mask and learning to forgive on *every* level.

The journey continues . . .

CHAPTER 11

Fork in the Road—Now What?

Forgiveness is not always easy. At times, it feels more painful than the wound we suffered, to forgive the one that inflicted it. And yet, there is no peace without forgiveness.

—**Marianne Williamson** [16]

My path of forgiveness has been anything but smooth. Instead, it has been an odyssey of walking up a descending escalator with what seemed like no end in sight, many times feeling like I was descending rather than moving upward.

When I look back at the wounds and emotional scars that my brothers and I suffered, it makes me think. For us four boys, there have been many forks in the road, times when we had to choose between living with the pain, shame, and blame that come from holding onto unforgiveness or taking the path to freedom through forgiveness.

Four brothers. Four paths. Four different outcomes.

Yes, there is a choice.

One brother, Jim, chose to hang on to the pain because it provided him a needed excuse to blame our dad for most every bad experience he had. Jim chose the path of hanging on to the pain because, to him, blaming Dad was easier and more comfortable than taking responsibility, taking control.

Unlike Jim, I choose to forgive our father, *not* because he deserved it but because I did.

While Jim did make some improvements toward the end of his life, sadly, his *Relational Credit Score* never got high enough for me to feel safe enough to reestablish our relationship before he passed away. Again, forgiveness does not require you to reconcile with your abuser or offender, especially if reconciling can put you back in harm's way.

> Can you identify with Jim? Is your life controlled by whatever wrong or painful thing that was done to you? For Jim, every mishap was *because* of our dad, as in, "I can't stop doing _____ *because* of what Dad did to me." Do you still perceive yourself as a victim instead of a former victim and have trouble letting go of hurt and anger? Is the mere thought of taking responsibility for your own emotional well-being too scary to even consider? Jim never let go of his anger, nor did he learn to forgive. As a consequence, his anger and hatred hurt himself and his family. His wound of unforgiveness was as toxic to his emotional well-being as hazardous chemicals are to our bodies. We must not use what was done to us as an excuse to continue the vicious cycle of hurt people hurting people.

Brother Bob chose the path of escape to quiet the pain and shame he felt. Like many men who have been abused, Bob donned a mask that leads to either (1) a cycle of quiet despair or (2) overcompensation. Bob did each at different times. Bob never allowed his mask to slip. It is said that people don't fake depression and bitterness; they fake being okay. He drowned out the voices of unforgiveness with booze and drugs until that fateful day when he took his own life.

Suicide doesn't take away the pain, it gives it to someone else. [17]

Bob's final act left behind a wife, two beautiful children, and many friends and family members to suffer grief, wondering what we could have been done differently. The level of pain he left behind to his family and friends can only be fully understood by those who have felt it firsthand.

> Can you identify with Bob? Do you bounce between overachievement and withdrawal? Are you kindhearted like Bob, and instead of revenge and reparations, you seek escape through alcohol, drugs, or ruminating over thoughts of suicide? You don't want to hurt anyone, but instead of moving on, do you turn that pain inward?

Brother Mike mentally checked out. He shields himself as much as possible from the outside world and his memories of years of abuse. To this day, he refuses to be touched; giving him a simple hug is out of the question. He escaped not by suicide but by putting up emotional walls to hide behind—his own personal prison of protection—only to discover that the walls he built trapped him inside his isolated world. Not surprisingly, Mike's path is one filled with loneliness, most of it the result of the barriers he has erected between himself and everyone else.

His path of isolation is safe and comfortable for him, and so that is where he stays: alive, but not fully living.

Mike's nightmares of our dad still haunt him to this day, and he strives to understand that if and when he can totally forgive, he, not his offender, will be the beneficiary.

> Can you identify with Mike? Do you struggle with anxiety and relive the pain over and over? Do you consciously—or unconsciously—prefer to live in your own fantasy world where you think you are protected from what happened to you or from it happening to you again? I suspect that deep down, Mike knows that his mental isolation can't keep him from pain, but it has caused him to miss out on so much of life.

I chose the path of forgiveness. As you have just read, on my path to forgiveness, I navigated many forks in the road. My journey is evidence that although the decisions along my path to decisional, emotional, and spiritual freedom were not easy to make, the benefits have been numerous: I have a happy life, and most of all, I no longer feel the need to wear the mask to hide my shame.

My path to forgiveness has been long and hard but worth the effort. My scars from the old wounds surface from time to time. But every day, I recommit to staying on the right path. Although my path has no finish line, let me encourage you by saying that my painful moments now occur far less frequently. And when they do appear, I'm better equipped to handle them.

> Can you identify with me? Do you seek freedom as much as someone dying of thirst seeks water or someone trapped underwater seeks air? If you yearn to be free from what has happened to you and are tormented by its associated anger, hate, blame, sorrow, depression, and, of course, shame, then forgiveness is the *only* path. Forgive those who have hurt or abused you, and join me to be free. Forgiveness is not easy. I get it. It often feels more painful than the wound we suffered. And yet, *there is no freedom without forgiveness.*

My Journey Is One of Hope, Understanding, and Freedom

You, too, have a choice. There is a fork in the road you are traveling. It's decision time.

Grim statistics show that one out of three to four women have been sexually abused. But did you know that one out of six men have been sexually abused as well?[18] How many of your male friends and coworkers are willing to own up to that? My point is this: in a broken world full of pain, shame, and blame, none of us gets through life completely unscathed.

If you were abused at some point, whether as a child, a teen, or as an adult, what happened to you was wrong, really wrong, and you have every right to hang on to that anger. Let's be honest: who really wants to forgive, especially when the offense was something horrible and the perpetrator doesn't deserve to be forgiven? Why should you even consider letting that person or persons off the hook? We men especially feel this way. We may talk about forgiveness, but what we really want is *justice*!

Forget reconciliation, we want reparations!

We feel as though we can't or shouldn't let our offender or abuser off the hook. We think that to do so is to let them get away with it, and that is neither good for society nor for the individuals involved in the offense. It feels like forgiving the abuser is to give something to someone who has already taken something from us. And that doesn't make any sense. After all, we are the ones who are owed.

And for those of us who are Christians, we often wonder, "Why do *we* have to repent and ask for forgiveness from God, yet our offender doesn't have to do the same to receive *our* forgiveness? That's not fair!" When we think of such things, we forget that there is a difference between asking to reconcile with God and forgiving others. We ask for God's forgiveness to reestablish a close relationship with Him; however, we forgive those who have hurt us to be *free from the results of the damage* they inflicted. Forgiving our abuser doesn't necessitate reconciliation with them. There is a big difference between reconciling with God and forgiving others to be free.

WISDOM AND INSIGHT FROM THIS CHAPTER

Many of us are the same way. We would rather fight to hold on to the blame because this blame has defined us. Without the pain caused by our offenders to define our actions, what are we? The path of forgiveness is often too scary for us to consider. We have ruminated over our offender for so long, often imagining all the punishments they so justly deserve, that taking the path to forgiveness can't be right; how could someone who has done so much wrong deserve to be forgiven? You deserve it because forgiving is one of the most liberating experiences you will ever have.

EPILOGUE

Freedom Found in Forgiveness

Some of the most generous people have no money. Some of the wisest people have no education. Some of the kindest people were hurt the most.

—**Steve Wentworth** [19]

When we hear a new word or concept, what do we do? We look up its meaning. However, there are words and concepts we've heard our whole life that we often mistakenly assume that we already know the meaning of. Unfortunately, sometimes assuming we know something can be more deceiving than not knowing it at all.

Let me share an illustration with you, a little story, to help you see where most of us have gone wrong on the subject of forgiveness. When you were young, do you remember your mom telling you to apologize to your brother or sister (or your parents themselves) for something you did wrong? What likely followed was an *exchange*, an apology asking for forgiveness. But let me ask you, were you really sorry? And did your sibling really believe you? Yet somehow, magically, this transaction took place, and it made everything all right and defined for you forever what forgiveness is all about

You were naturally led to believe for you to forgive, the other party needs to apologize and make amends. And *only* when that happened were the scales of justice once again in balance—whatever debt that existed was now paid. There must be an exchange for forgiveness to exist.

You see, most people don't understand what forgiveness is really about.

Looking Deeper at Forgiveness

As evidenced in my forgiveness journey and contrary to popular belief, forgiveness is a one-sided transaction only—it does not take two. Even though there seem to be two sides—the person who was hurt and the person who inflicted the hurt—forgiveness is solely subject to the offended, not the offender.

Forgiveness does not depend on the offender paying us back—in whole or in part—especially since we are talking about a debt that usually can never be repaid. What could my dad have ever said to balance the scales of justice and make it right?

Forgiveness is also not subject to the offender issuing an apology. Heck, forgiveness is not even subject to their being reachable or even alive! They could be long out of your life, but you can still forgive them. You could know them intimately, or they could be a total stranger.

Instead, forgiveness is about your choosing to cancel a debt, and that is exactly what I did. You can choose to continue to hang on to this debt if you wish, but in doing so, you have no choice but to accept the accompanied feelings of resentment, pain, and shame.

Simply put, forgiveness is *only* about your side. It has nothing to do with the offender. Forgiveness is not:

- Subject to their knowing the pain they caused us
- Subject to an apology

- Subject to retribution

In short, my friends, forgiveness needs *nothing* from them. You can free yourself.

In reality, saying or hearing "I forgive you" or "I'm sorry" has *little to do with real forgiveness*. We see this in adults when they utter such words as "I forgave them, but if their house burnt down, it would serve them right!" That doesn't sound like the emotional and spiritual freedom that comes from canceling a debt, does it?

This kind of thinking comes from the fact that something was taken or broken, and now a debt exists that needs to be repaid. This is the definition of justice, pure and simple—the need to balance the scale and make everything right. It often includes the offender paying some sort of price and getting what they deserve (in the form of a punishment).

When we view forgiving others in a transactional sense, we, of course, can't let our offenders off the hook because to do so is to let them get away with what they did. And yet this transactional view of forgiveness, where we even the scales, doesn't leave us satisfied. At times, thinking of forgiveness as a transaction keeps us from wanting to forgive because there is no punishment they could suffer that feels like an equal repayment for our pain.

Rather than wait for those who have wronged you to take responsibility for their actions, you have the ability to take the wheel back in your life. You can choose to resist the temptation to be a passive observer as your offender continues to steer your life in painful directions. They made you a victim; why allow them to continue to do so?

It also doesn't help that every time something bad happens, the public conversation turns quickly to *"Who is responsible?"* and *"They need to pay for this."*

The truth is none of us can ever balance the scales of justice. Thinking that our forgiveness needs to be subject to our offender making things right or paying a price for what they did or even some kind of balancing of the scales isn't going to get us the result we are looking for.

So, if you are waiting for an equal payback as a prerequisite to forgive, more often than not, the payback is not only insufficient, but the mere attempt can make you angrier since it falls short of the retribution that you have ruminated upon for so long. As previously mentioned, what could my dad have ever said or done to make it right or even the scales of justice? Nothing.

In the end, if we want to experience the freedom of forgiving our abuser or offender, we have to abandon this transactional concept.

By definition, forgiveness is a conscious, deliberate decision to release feelings of resentment or vengeance toward a person, yourself, or a group who has harmed you, *regardless of whether they deserve it*. Again, forgiving requires nothing from the person being forgiven. Think about it.

Forgiveness Does Not Ignore What Happened

Even though my forgiveness did not require my abusers to ask for forgiveness, my own healing, freedom, and forgiveness *did not downplay or ignore the offense*; in fact, it's quite the opposite. I appeal to you to accept and account for all the pain that was caused and to allow yourself to fully grieve and document that pain. Granted, it hurt to open up the wounds so they could finally heal properly, but the step of accounting for all the pain had to take place so that I knew exactly what I was forgiving.

Forgiveness at any level does not necessarily mean that you will go back to the way you were before you were wounded. There will be a scar.

Somedays my scars still hurt. Just as physical scars act as reminders of experiences we don't want to repeat, emotional scars, when healed, can act as warning signs to steer us away from unforgiveness. Even with the healing power of forgiveness, certain sounds, songs, smells, or situations can trigger a memory of the trauma. But the healing power of forgiveness means that there is no emotional pain attached to that memory. That memory has no power to affect and infect me or my relationships.

As they say at Alcoholics Anonymous, "Once you become a pickle, you will never be a cucumber again."

What if you could forgive that hurt and injustice so you don't have to carry it around another day?

I get it. I understand the resistance. *They* don't deserve it, but *you* do.

Doing it for *you* is a great first step. However, doing it for yourself will yield only a limited amount of good.

Forgiveness is a gift to the offender that benefits the offended. Many studies on the science of forgiveness conclude that much more benefit comes from practicing forgiveness as an altruistic gift to the offender rather than doing it solely for yourself. [20] Because you are in the unique position of the one who was harmed, you are likewise in a unique position to give this gift, and it is through giving this gift that many of your most cherished, long-term benefits come.

In my journey, the biggest payoff of freedom from the pain, shame, and blame came when I took off my mask and truly forgave my dad and those cowboys in Wyoming. Who won with that? I did!

Think of forgiveness as a gift, an altruistic gift to your offender. Forgiving is for giving.

Start with Hope

When you decide that you want to forgive your offender and be free, where do you start? The first step is to have hope because where there is no hope, there is only despair. Embrace the knowledge that you can do this and feel hopeful. You can live in a world where you don't have to carry that anger, resentment, and shame around with you anymore. You can be happy and feel worthy regardless of what you went through.

Escaping my awful past and living a better life all started with hope.

Does that promise of a better life, like I've had, sound enticing enough for you to take these steps?

We are not intrinsically wired to want to forgive, but we are wired to desire freedom, and we can move forward on the journey to forgiving if we hope and aim for freedom!

Understanding and Accounting of What Happened

When you consider what has happened to you, it's time for you to make an accounting of what happened, how it hurt, and what were the downstream consequences. I know that it hurts to dredge up all those uncomfortable feelings, but be specific. Just like an accounting of monetary debt that we would be asking to write off, ponder exactly what it is that you are forgiving.

Vividly recall the hurt and consider writing it down. The pain of revisiting the hurt, including all the subsequent damage it caused in your life, is an important step of accounting for all that you are forgiving. Ask any accountant: if you are going to write off a debt, you will need to be both honest and specific.

This step prompted me to want to forgive even more—others and myself. I started to write down every transgression from others *and* those I've done myself. I contacted family members and friends from my childhood to uncover any details I might have missed or blocked out. In doing so, it was painful to discover that my dad had done even worse things than I remembered. If I was going to forgive it all and truly write off the debt, I wanted to conduct a *complete* accounting.

Regardless of asking for or granting forgiveness, it's best to include more than just the offense but also the pain it caused and the consequences. Before you sit down to begin this task, recall the important step that must be done first: the accounting.

For example:

1) I totally forgive them for hitting my arm with a bat. I totally do so. I fully acknowledge it was wrong (*what happened*).
2) I totally forgive them for breaking my arm (*the damage caused*).
3) I totally forgive them for causing me to miss the golf tournament I had been wanting to play for the past year (*the consequences*).

If you have a full accounting and can cover all three points of forgiveness, then you are ready to proceed. Let's apply that to you now:

1) Make a full accounting—write it down if you need to do so.
    a. Account for what they really did; be honest and specific.
    b. Account in full for the damage it caused.
    c. Account in full for the consequences it caused, including later in life.
2) Forgive: "I totally forgive them for [what they did] and the [damage it caused], resulting in [consequences]."

If you are comfortable holding onto your pain and are not yet ready to let go of it, I understand. Whatever happened to you, you have every right to hold on to and identify with that pain. If responsibility for your emotional well-being may be too scary for you, I get it.

But if you are tired and your shoulders are exhausted from carrying around your backpack of pain, shame, and blame, then I am here to tell you there is hope. When you finally tire of wearing a mask to hide the real you from others, there is a much more fulfilling alternative. If enough is enough and you want to be free, then there is a path.

That path is forgiveness. Even though forgiveness can't change your *past*, it can and will change your *future*.

Shame

When you look in the mirror, do you see a failure? A loser? Do you desire to be convinced that God and others can really love all of who you really are? Do you hide your true self, inner conflicts, failures, regrets, and shame? How can God bless someone who has done, and sometimes is still doing, such bad things? Do you believe that you're not worthy and that others would reject you if they knew the real you?

Or do you desire to one day look into the mirror and with conviction say, "I am enough"? Moreover, "I like myself, and others truly want me, despite who I am, despite what happened to me, and despite what I did!"

When we don't open up to others, stop being so self-judgmental, and begin to forgive, our shame-filled past becomes our shame-filled future. But when we release our shame-filled past and forgive ourselves and others, we experience peace and a level of self-worth that we never thought possible.

Brené Brown has defined shame like this:

It is the intensely painful feeling or experience of believing that we are flawed and therefore unworthy of love and belonging. It's an emotion that affects all of us and profoundly shapes the way we interact in the world. [21]

As I shared previously, shame requires three things to exist:

- Secrecy
- Judgment
- Unforgiveness

Remove them, and shame ceases to thrive. The shame is reinforced *if you keep your story or issue to yourself*. Keeping the unforgiveness hidden feeds the shame. Keeping the shame silent in the dark makes it grow. Expose it to the light of day, however, and it loses its power over you. It is only when you explore your darkness that you will discover the light of freedom found in forgiveness.

For the readers who are Christians, regardless of what you did, the shame you feel for it, or how you see yourself, you are already perfected in God's eyes. What if you could look into the mirror and see yourself as God sees you? You are the righteousness of God just as you are!

> God made him who had no sin to be sin for us, so that in Him *we might become the righteousness of God*. —2 Corinthians 5:21 (NIV)

> Therefore, there is now *no* condemnation for those who are in Christ Jesus." —Romans 8:1 (NIV)

Forgiving Prayer

I hope and pray that you can see forgiveness under new optics as freedom rather than a transaction. My promise to you is as you do so, you will be released from your pain, shame, and blame, and these will be replaced with hope, understanding, and freedom!

As a last word, I want to share with you this helpful prayer. You are under no obligation to use it, but I hope that it can help you frame forgiveness properly.

Lord, <*my offender*> **injured me by** <*name the injustice of what happened*>.

Because of this, I experienced <*name the damage*> **and** <*name the resulting consequences*>.

I have held this debt too long.

Just as You have forgiven me; I choose to forgive them.

I do not condone or excuse what they did—it was wrong, and I was wronged.

However, I want to be free in my head, my heart, my soul, and in my emotions.

I choose to release this debt. <*name the offender*> **doesn't owe me anything.**

I release <*offender*>**'s debt completely, without question and without any payback.**

Right now, at this moment, I choose to be free. I forgive them *completely*.

About the Author

Mark Goodman is the executive director of the forgiveness and reconciliation nonprofit 70x7.org. Mark's personal story has taken him from an abusive home life in Detroit to being homeless on the streets of LA. Through this journey, Mark personally benefited from the freedom found in forgiveness. Mark founded 70x7.org, a faith-based nonprofit, to aid people who are hanging on to pain, shame, and blame from past hurt and to help them on their path to forgiveness.

Mark's mission in forgiveness and reconciliation is unique because it combines data-driven studies with input from clinical psychology, theology, and real-life experiences.

If you have a forgiveness story to share or a message for the author, you can reach Mark at markgoodman@70x7.org.

Additional Resources

If you are a victim of physical or sexual abuse, contact the National Domestic Hotline at 800-799-7233.

70x7—Path to Forgiveness (70x7.org). Nonprofit for additional information on how to forgive, founded by the author, Mark Goodman.

The Forgiveness Project (theforgivenessproject.com). Personal stories of forgiveness.

TheHotline.org. Free and confidential.

1 in 6 (1in6.org). Nonprofit to assist men who have been through sexual abuse.

Joyful Heart Foundation (joyfulheartfoundation.org). Nonprofit founded by Mariska Hargitay of *Law & Order: Special Victims Unit* to transform society's response to sexual assault, domestic violence, and child abuse and support survivor's healing.

BetterHelp (betterhelp.com). World's largest online therapy assistance.

Suggested books to read to learn more about forgiveness and reconciliation:

Practicing Forgiveness: How to Forgive, Reconcile, and Restore Relationships (Audible only) by Everett Worthington

Handbook of Forgiveness by Everett Worthington and Nathaniel Wade

Psychology of Achievement by Brian Tracy

70x7: Forgiving Your Abusers by Scott Green

Live to Forgive by Jason Romano

Boundaries by Dr. Henry Cloud and Dr. John Townsend

Forgiveness: An Exploration by Marina Cantacuzino

Good Boundaries and Goodbyes by Lysa TerKeurst

Notes

(1) 1868, Josh Billings on *Ice, and Other Things* by Josh Billings (Henry Wheeler Shaw), Chapter 24: Perkussion Caps, Quote Page 89 and 80, G. W. Carleton & Company, New York

(2) Quote from *The Gifts of Imperfection* by Brené Brown, 10th Edition, Hazelden Publishing, page 6, March 2022.

(3) William P. Young interview with NPR related to writing his book, *The Shack*. https://www.npr.org/2012/12/01/166026305/cross-roads-a-writing-career-built-on-faith

(4) National WW2 Museum, Okinawa: The Cost of Victory in the Last Battle, July 7, 2022. https://www.nationalww2museum.org/war/articles/okinawa-costs-victory-last-battle

(5) Email from Mike Goodman to Mark Goodman, August 13, 2019.

(6) Quote from Andy Defresne, played by Tim Robbins, in the movie Shawshank Redemption, 1994, written by Stephen King.

(7) Quote by Cheryl Hunter from her TEDxSantaMonica talk, Wabi-Sabi: The Magnificence of Imperfection. March 21, 2103.

(8) Quote from Abhysheq Shukla from Feelings Undefined: The Charm of the Unsaid Vol 1, Createspace, April 11, 2017.

(9) Quote from Ziad K. Abdelnour from Economic Warfare: Secrets of Wealth Creation in the Age of Welfare Politics, Wiley, December 27, 2011.

(10) Quote often credited to Mark Twain but actually from Lucius Annaeus Seneca the Younger (4 BC – AD 65). His work defines and explains anger within the context of Stoic philosophy, and offers therapeutic advice on what to do to prevent anger.

(11) Often miscredited to C.S. Lewis, this is a quote from an unknown author in the book Chicken Soup for the Soul: Think Possible by Amy Newmark and Deborah Norville, Simon & Schuster, October 6, 2015.

(12) Quote from Brené Brown from Royal Society of the Arts video short titled Brené Brown on Shame, February 3, 2015.

(13) Author unknown although commonly cited to Zig Ziglar.

(14) Quote from The Cure by John Lynch, Bruce McNikol, and Bill Thrall, Chapter 2, Published by CrossSection, First Edition, October 2011.

(15) John Lynch Speaks, Part 2: I Have Been Completely Changed, March 9, 2020. https://www.johnlynchspeaks.com/content-blog/06s436y7j8p52p5et33bt2psnk3ahp

(16) Chang, L. (2006). *Wisdom for the soul: Five Millennia of Prescriptions for Spiritual Healing.* Gnosophia Publishers.

(17) Quote from David Foster Wallace, Charity Navigator, Facebook post on February 19, 2019. https://www.facebook.com/charitynavigator/posts/suicide-doesnt-take-away-the-pain-it-gives-it-to-someone-else-david-foster-walla/10157022089638781

(18) Statistics from 1in6 (1in6.org)

(19) Steve Wentworth Facebook post, March 11, 2021.

(20) Handbook of Forgiveness 2nd Edition, Everett L. Worthington Jr. and Nathaniel G. Wade, Published 2020, Routledge, page 278.

(21) Daring Greatly, Brené Brown, Penguin Publishing Group, April 7, 2015.

Printed in the USA
CPSIA information can be obtained
at www.ICGtesting.com
CBHW061716071123
1736CB00008B/121